BLACK TERROR

BY
RICHARD WESLEY

★

★

DRAMATISTS
PLAY SERVICE
INC.

The New York production of BLACK TERROR opened at the Public Theater in the fall of 1971. The production was directed by Nathan George; the set design was by Marjorie Kellogg, and the lighting design was by Buddy Butler. The cast was as follows:

ANTAR .... Paul Benjamin
AHMED .... Kirk Young
KEUSI .... Gylan Kain
M'BALIA .... Susan Batson
GERONIMO .... Don Blakely
RADCLIFFE .... Earl Sydnor
DANCER .... Dolores Vanison
PRIESTESS .... Freda Vanderpool
BROTHERS AND SISTERS INVOLVED
IN THE STRUGGLE .... Preston Bradley, Niger Akoni,
James Buckley, Sylvia Soares
MUSICIANS .... Babafemi Akinlana, Ralph Dorsey,
Ladji Camara

Notes on *Black Terror*

I began thinking about writing a play about the "revolutionary phase" of the post-Civil Rights struggle after a series of national incidents made me question the efficacy of armed resistance as a means of protest and an engine of change.

In 1966, the Spanish film director Gillo Pontecorvo directed a landmark film entitled *The Battle of Algiers*. The film takes place during the 1950s and is set in the Kasbah, the segregated Arab quarter of Algiers, the capital of French-occupied Algeria. Mr. Pontecorvo's picture presented a fictionalized account of the first insurrection against French colonial rule and showed how, though ultimately unsuccessful, that insurrection led directly to the struggle for Algerian independence. The French were overwhelmed by the end of the decade, and this led to a newly independent Algeria in the early '60s. Shot in a semi-documentary style, in grainy black and white, the film had a major influence on young liberation militants the world over, not the least in the United States, where youthful black men and women compared life in the Kasbah with life in the inner cities of their own country. Ultimately, many young people began to wonder if the "lessons" of *The Battle of Algiers* could not be applied to the armed struggle at home. Such conversations were held among young people in private parties, across tables in smoky cafés, on street corners, and even in college classrooms on campuses across the United States. And not just black kids, but white and Latino and Native American as well—everywhere the film was shown, oppressed and suppressed people were sure to begin drawing parallels.

However, my own response to the film, while very much appreciating its sentiments, was muted because of one particular memory. Not too long before seeing Pontecorvo's film, I was called into the Homicide Division of the Newark Police Department to answer questions. It turned out that a friend I had worked with in a program sponsored by HARYOU-ACT, an anti-poverty agency based in Harlem, had been found shot to death in a rooming house. My name was among his belongings, and the police were seeking out everyone who knew him to determine any leads.

As I sat there speaking to a detective, my eye couldn't help but take in my surroundings. What stood out for me were the street maps on the walls and their level of detail: alleys, dead ends, the locations of police boxes—they were all there. The memory of those maps came back to me as I noticed the way the French commander depicted in *Battle of Algiers* used similar maps to track down and defeat the Algerian militants. It would also come back to me two years later, as I read about the police raid on the Black Panther Party headquarters in Los Angeles.

Fred Hampton was a young, charismatic leader of the Chicago branch of the Black Panther Party. He was twenty-one years old, handsome, athletic, intelligent, and erudite. If ever there was an heir apparent to Huey Newton, the party's by-then-imprisoned national leader, it was Fred Hampton—even more so than the party's internationally known minister of defense, Eldridge Cleaver. Hampton was assassinated in his bed by members of the Chicago and Illinois police. The world would later learn that he had been betrayed by an informant who was in the employ of the FBI, and that the operation was just one more offshoot of their COINTELPRO (or counterintelligence program), designed to delay, disrupt, and ultimately destroy any and all "militant" movements or operations within the African-American community.

A group of young white sympathizers of the then-nascent Weather Underground were sharing an apartment in a Greenwich Village brownstone in New York City. They had become radicalized by what they saw happening to the Black Panther Party, the slow but steady dismantling of the war on poverty by the Nixon Administration, efforts by the CIA to undermine or destroy leftist liberation movements across the Third World, and, foremost, by their deeply felt opposition to the United States' expansion of the war in Vietnam. These young people were secretly making bombs in their apartment when, inexplicably, one of the bombs blew up. It destroyed virtually the entire building and killed all of the young people save one, Bernardine Dohrn, who was seen bloodied, naked, and in shock, fleeing the rubble. She would remain on the FBI's Most Wanted list for nearly thirty years before voluntarily turning herself in during the Clinton administration.

Out on the West Coast, political tensions had arisen between the Black Panther Party—Marxist-influenced and politically aligned with a loose and racially mixed amalgam of domestic and foreign leftist political movements—and US, a Black Nationalist organization that eschewed such political alliances in favor of total commitment to, and concentration within, the African-American community. Those political differences—coupled with an ever-growing dependence on guns as a means of both defense and of imposing the political will of members of the Los Angeles chapter of the Black Panther Party and the Los Angeles chapter of US—ultimately led to violent confrontations between members of these organizations, escalating to such intensity that the leadership on both sides attempted to arrange a meeting to effect a truce and dial down the temperature. One such meeting was supposed to occur in a cafeteria on the campus of UCLA. Instead, gunfire erupted and two Panthers were killed. A pall was cast over the entire Black Liberation movement and remained for years to come; some might say it never lifted.

The LAPD attempted a raid on the Los Angeles headquarters of the Black Panther Party during the summer of 1970. A sixteen-square-block area around the building was cordoned off; residents were ordered to remain in their homes and off the streets. The police used an armored car (similar to the one featured in the original *Die Hard* movie), and all of the officers were armed with AR-15s, the civilian version of the M-15s U.S. troops were using in the bush and marshes of Vietnam. It turned out, however, that the Panthers had fortified their headquarters, and they resisted the superior firepower of the police for a number of hours before surrendering when their ammo ran out. There were fewer than ten Panthers inside, some of them young women. When I heard the news, I thought again about those street maps in the Newark Police Headquarters building.

And then Huey Newton, in an article in the Black Panther Party newspaper, introduced and advocated the idea of "the urban kamikaze"—revolutionary guerrillas, on suicide missions, prepared to sacrifice all for the movement. It was a notion that was quickly abandoned, but for me it was a clear declaration that the armed faction of the Black Liberation movement had finally run out of ideas.

I was determined to say something. I decided, finally, to put "the Revolution" onstage, to write a play that would take place "in the very near future, given the nature of American society." I wanted a play in which all of the ideas about armed struggle, and the unquestioning fealty to nationalist as well as leftist ideals, would be presented not as possibilities but as fact; my characters would exemplify and live out these ideals before our eyes, and they would execute the armed struggle.

The stage would serve as a laboratory, allowing the audience to determine, through the dramatic presentation of ideas in action, whether the revolution that was being waged in their name needed to be changed, improved, executed exactly as it was, or abandoned.

I began work on the play almost immediately after the raid on the Los Angeles Black Panther Party headquarters. I collected newspaper articles and photographs of the raid and studied them daily. Ed Bullins, one of the finest playwrights in the country at the time, loaned me a book he'd bought on a trip to London: *Zero*, about the Nihilist movement in nineteenth-century Europe. I learned how the Czar of Russia had ordered his secret police to wage a counterintelligence operation that not only infiltrated the various Nihilist cells in Russia, but also fomented dissent, ran smear campaigns against the leadership, took over cells and ran them, and functioned as informants. The resemblance to the FBI's COINTELPRO was unmistakable.

I attended symposia on art and politics in Harlem, Brooklyn's Bedford-Stuyvesant, and Newark, New Jersey, and every day, every spare minute I had, I was writing—a sentence here, a scene there—all by hand, on a yellow legal pad that I carried in a military map bag slung over my shoulder. I wrote at home, on the bus to visit my then-girlfriend, on the subway to work, at parties, and backstage at the New Lafayette Theatre where I was managing editor of *Black Theatre Magazine*, until finally, some six months after I began, the play was completed. I settled on the title *Black Terror* because I knew it was provocative and people would come to see it. I intended to write a play that could be performed in gymnasiums, on portable stages in open parks, in the quadrangles of housing developments—plays for the people, where the largest number of people were most likely to be. I also knew that designing a play that could be performed in the community, particularly a play that carried the message this one did, meant that the primary audience for *Terror* would be those who would most suffer the consequences of an armed struggle in the streets of America.

Terror's first public exposure was a reading in the Black Theatre Workshop, headed by Ed Bullins. Later, a former Howard University classmate, Rafique Bey, presented *Terror* as his thesis play. The FBI, which had already been on campus to observe student activism protesting the Vietnam War and support of Black Nationalist leaders on campus, attended in large numbers. At the same time, Ed Bullins showed the play to producer Joseph Papp, artistic director of the New York Shakespeare Festival/Public Theater. Papp—himself an old-school activist from the '30s and '40s—immediately took a liking to *Black Terror*, reached out to me, and made a commitment to producing the play in his theater, where it opened in October 1971.

—R. W.

BROTHERS AND SISTERS
INVOLVED IN THE STRUGGLE

ANTAR—Late twenties or early thirties. College education. Strong, well-muscled, and stern. Relatively quiet. Speaks in soft tones. Not given to boisterousness.

AHMED—Somewhat younger. Full of fire. Could be a good leader if he would calm down and check things out.

KEUSI—Full name, Keusi Kifo ("Black Death"). He is in his mid- to late twenties and is a war vet. He is always a man who knows whereof he speaks.

M'BALIA—Named for M'Balia Camara, a Black woman who is known in Africa as a woman whose death was one of the sparks of the Guinean drive for independence from France. The sister is strong, determined, and a devoted revolutionary. She is not unfeminine, but displays her womanness only when she feels it suits her.

GERONIMO—A fiery revolutionary. Leader of the local chapter of the American Liberation Front. Quick-tempered; a flair for the dramatic. At times he seems almost unreal.

CHAUNCEY RADCLIFFE—Middle-aged. A moderate Black man who thinks he is doing the right thing.

OTHERS—Three brothers, a sister, other members of the Black Terrorists, and white-sounding voices coming in over the radio.

PLACE

The setting will alternate between the Terrorist headquarters, a tenement apartment, and the home of Dr. Chauncey Radcliffe.

TIME

The very near future, given the nature of American society.

BLACK TERROR

Scene 1

Blood-red lights on a dark chamber. A number of young Black revolutionaries are gathered to perform a ceremony. Drums are playing. The women sing in eerie, high-pitched voices; the men make grunting and moaning sounds that blend in with the voices of the women. Bodies are swaying. Dancing. The smell of incense is in the air. A fire burns at an altar, Antar stands in front of the altar. The music, singing, and dances build to a frenzy until Antar bids silence. Ahmed, standing nearby, steps forward, raises clenched fist.

AHMED. We are the Black Terrorists, sworn to the liberation of our people.

ALL. May we never lose sight of our duty.

AHMED. We seek the death of those who oppress us.

ALL. May our vengeance be as swift as lightning.

AHMED. We are the Black Terrorists, sworn to uphold the dignity of our African bloodline.

ALL. May we suffer death before disgrace to our ancestors.

AHMED. We live by the will of the Supreme Black Spirit to create a world of peace and beauty after the revolution.

ALL. May the blood of our oppressors never cease to flow until that world is realized.

AHMED. We are the Black Terrorists, sworn to die for the liberation of our people.

ALL. The oppressor of our people must die! We shall kill him where he works, we shall kill him as he sleeps, we shall kill him wherever he is. He must know of the wrath that befalls those who

11

consider themselves above the laws of God and humanity. His death will free our nation! His death will free the world! AAAAAA AAAAAAIIIIIIIIIIIIIEEEEEEEEEEEEEE!!!!!!!!!

> *Drums. Wild dancing. Women dancing. Men shuffling in place. Shouting and screaming. Chants are heard. Silence as Antar raises his hands.*

ANTAR. Bring in the candidate.

> *Two young Terrorists escort Keusi to the altar. Drum is heard softly in the background. Keusi kneels before Antar and altar.*

Ndugu Keusi Kifo, you kneel before me having been chosen by vote to carry out a mission of assassination against the most vicious and ruthless enemy of the people in this area. Your target is Police Commissioner Charles Savage, organizer of the mad-dog Night Rangers of the police department. He is an avowed enemy of the revolution and he is therefore an oppressor. He must die.

ALL. *(Chant.)*

> Lasima Tuchinde Mbilishaka!
> Lasima Tuchinde Mbilishaka!
> Lasima Tuchinde Mbilishaka!

> *M'Balia will come forward from the assembly and kneel at the altar before Keusi.*

(Sing.)

> Spirits of our forefathers
> Come forth
> Reach into our hearts
> And remove the fear
> Reach into our minds
> And remove the doubt
> Release the anger in our souls
> And give us strength
> To do
> What must
> Be done.

(Chant.)

> Sifa Ote Mtu Weusi

Sifa Ote Mtu Weusi
Sifa Ote Mtu Weusi

ANTAR. Dada M'Balia, you kneel before me, having volunteered to team with Ndugu Keusi in the execution of this mission. Your past performances in action have proven you to be an outstanding revolutionary and an expert terrorist. Your knowledge and experience will prove to be the perfect complement to Ndugu Keusi's own revolutionary talents.

> *The others will sing the lines below as Antar is given a large knife by Ahmed. He places the knife in a fire on the altar to purify it. Antar holds the knife aloft. Drums grow louder, then subside. Antar takes Keusi's arm and makes an incision, then does the same with M'Balia. Meanwhile, the others are singing.*

ALL. *(Sing.)*
Spirits of the Black Nation
Come.
Take hold of your servants
Guide our lives
Make us strong
Place steel in the marrow of our bones
Grant us inner peace
To fulfill our terrible missions.
(Chant.)
Lasima Tuchinde Mbilishaka
Lasima Tuchinde Mbilishaka
Lasima Tuchinde Mbilishaka

ANTAR. Ndugu Keusi and Dada M'Balia, the two of you have been joined together by blood. Until this mission is complete or until I terminate this mission, you will guard each other with your lives.

> *Ahmed steps forward with an array of weapons on a dark red pillow.*

You will assume secret identities and live within the community and await the opportune moment to carry out your orders.

> *Hands weapons to Keusi.*

These are your weapons. You will use them well, my brother. What say you both?

KEUSI and M'BALIA. *(In an incantation.)* Spirit Guardians of the dark regions
Hear my cry
Let not my will falter
Let not my desire fall
With all my strength
Let me defeat my enemy
With all my soul
Let me defeat my enemy
Let me see to the will of
The Black Nation
Show me
No mercy
Should I fail my
Sacred oath.

AHMED. *(Steps forward, raises clenched fist.)* We are the Black Terrorists, sworn to the liberation of our people.

ALL. May we never lose sight of our duty.

AHMED. We seek the death of those who oppress us.

ALL. May our vengeance be as swift as lightning. AAAAAAAA AAAIIIIEEEEEEEEEEEEE!!!!!!!

> *Drum, music, dancing as Keusi and M'Balia exit. Lights go down.*

Scene 2

> *Lights up on a room in a tenement apartment. Very little furniture. Large rug on the floor. Keusi, M'Balia, and Ahmed sit on large cushions.*

AHMED. All right, listen up. Ndugu Keusi, your target has a set pattern of behavior. He plays golf at the Golden Triangle every weekend from 11 A.M. to 5 P.M. He showers, then leaves the golf course promptly at 6:45 P.M. He always takes the parkway back to the city.

KEUSI. He travel alone?

AHMED. Always. Now, about twenty-five miles south of the city, the parkway has this big curve in it that goes through this valley. There are a lot of trees, high grass, and shrubbery. He usually hits that curve around 7:15. And he drives in the left lane.

KEUSI. What kinda car do he drive?

AHMED. (Piqued.) Man, didn't you study the briefing notes on the target?

KEUSI. Yeah, well, I don't remember seeing anything in it about the kinda car he got.

AHMED. It was in there, man. Dammit, man. Get yourself together. You blow this mission—

KEUSI. (Annoyed.) Just tell me what kinda car he drive. I don't need no lecture.

AHMED. You better watch your mouth, man. You still only an initiate. One word from me and your ass'll be crawling in the dirt.

KEUSI. I'm sorry, man. Nervous, I guess.

AHMED. Don't be sorry, just keep in mind your position when you talk to someone who got rank over you. Now, in view of the fact that you ain't studied, I gotta take time out to get up off a whole lotta insignificant information. The target drives a 1965 Buick LeSabre; four-door; blue. License plate number NPD-911.

    Keusi writes info down.

KEUSI. Got it. Thanks, man.

AHMED. (Ignoring him.) It's important that you be on the right-hand slope of the valley at 7:15 to get the best shot at the target. The high grass will hide you. We figure once the oppressor is hit his car will veer out of control and crash. In the confusion, you can make a sure getaway. Be sure you can find the ejected shell and take it with you. We don't want no clues left behind, at all.

KEUSI. Aw, man, now how the hell am I gonna find an ejected shell in all that grass?

AHMED. Look, stop questioning your orders and do like you're told. All the FBI gotta do is find a shell, or some other seemingly insignificant shit, and the next thing you know they'll be banging on our door.

KEUSI. They ain't gonna find us behind no goddamn shell.

AHMED. Stop questioning your orders and do like you told.

KEUSI. Yeah. Okay, I'm sorry. You got anything else to tell me?

AHMED. No. That's it. The rest is in your notes.

KEUSI. Yeah, okay, I got a question. This shit sound too risky. Have y'all got an alternate plan?

AHMED. Yeah, but it's more difficult 'cause you got to eliminate your target in front of his home. The target is pretty much a loner. He's a bachelor, so he lives alone in his house. He got very few real close friends and seldom gets visitors. His house is at 631 Peachtree Drive, near Talmadge Avenue. He works a sixteen-hour day and usually gets home about 9:30 at night. Usually all the lights in his house go out around 11:30, so we figure that must be about the time he goes to bed. Observation shows that he usually gets outta his house by 7:30 A.M. The best time, then, to eliminate him is between 9:30 at night and 7:30 in the morning. There's a park across the street from where he lives. Lotsa trees and good cover. Ideal for a mission like yours.

KEUSI. Yeah, I like that. A park. Nighttime. Good cover. Hell, yeah, I like that idea. I'll probably do the job at Savage's house rather than on that stupid highway. Shit, why not?

AHMED. Where you eliminate your target doesn't matter. The idea is to execute your mission clearly, efficiently, and without the possibility of detection. Complete your assignment by the end of the week.

KEUSI. It'll be done.

AHMED. *(To M'Balia.)* Have you any suggestions or amendments, my sister?

M'BALIA. No. Y'all the men. I trust your ideas.

AHMED. Okay, then it's all set. Good. I've got to leave, 'cause Antar and I got things to discuss.

    All rise, they move to door.

A word of caution, Ndugu Keusi Kifo. Your mouth is too big, man. You got the makings of a damn good revolutionary, but you try to think too much. You know? Don't think. Let your leaders do the

16

thinking. That's their job. Your job is to do or die. Remember that. Okay?

> *Keusi smiles and nods. Ahmed and Keusi shake hands. Then Ahmed embraces and kisses M'Balia on both cheeks.*

Good luck to you both.

KEUSI. Yeah, man, thanks.

M'BALIA. Asante, Ndugu Ahmed.

AHMED. Kwaheri.

KEUSI. Later.

M'BALIA. Kwaheri, Ndugu Ahmed.

> *Ahmed exits.*

KEUSI. Jive-ass motherfucker. I wouldn't follow him across the goddamn street.

> *M'Balia looks at him very hard.*

Well, it's all set. That's good.

M'BALIA. I'd better go and clean your weapon.

KEUSI. Hold it a minute. I'm not so sure I wanna use that rifle.

M'BALIA. *(Harshly.)* What do you propose to use then? A knife? Your hands? You could fail if you try those methods. The revolution can't afford any failures, Ndugu Kifo.

KEUSI. I'm hip to that, M'Balia, but look at it from this angle. Out on the parkway, if I got to take aim and fire in all that high grass, how the hell am I gonna know where the spent shell falls? I could be up there for days looking for some goddamn shell just so the FBI don't have too many clues. I could get caught up there looking for that shell. And that park across from where Savage lives. It's in a white neighborhood. I'm gonna have a helluva time even gettin' into that area. Then fire a high-powered rifle. The sound of the shot is gonna bring people. Someone's bound to see me running. Of course, I could put cushioning and wire mesh around the barrel and chamber of the gun to muffle the sound of the shot, but then there's the problem of the gun flash. Suppose I need more than one shot—highly unlikely as good as I am, but possible anyway— suppose I need more than one shot, people are bound to see the gun flash. It's warm out, there gonna be people all over the place.

Then, 'cause I shouldn't question orders, I gotta crawl around in the dark lookin' for some stupid-ass shell. After I do that, I gotta worry about gettin' my Black behind outta there with cops crawlin' all over the place lookin' for the sniper who offed the pig. Naw, there got to be an easier way. I don't wanna wind up a martyr on my first mission.

M'BALIA. We know it is risky, Ndugu Keusi, but you should realize that the success of your mission overrides any consideration of the success of your escape. You should not expect to survive the revolution. As an initiate to the Black Terrorists that realization will be some time in coming. But as you become more of a part of us, you will accept that point of view as a reality.

KEUSI. I don't accept the inevitability of a revolutionary death. Understand? He who assassinates and gets away shall live to assassinate another day—if he's clever. And I intend to be clever. I ain't hardly suicidal.

M'BALIA. No one asked you to be. You have an assignment to carry out. You will not shirk your duty.

KEUSI. I ain't shirkin' no duty. I'm just tellin' you that to kill this man there must be a simpler way just as efficient as a gun that won't give me the problems I mentioned before. I know I'll think of something. Just give me some time. Commissioner Savage will not see the weekend. Imagine, he's walkin' around thinking about his golf game this weekend, not knowing that there's a nigger right now thinking of offing him before he even gets one stroke in. Life is funny like that. One minute everything is cool, the next minute, CRASH!!!! Just like that it's all over. Too bad. I almost feel sorry for that old bastard.

M'Balia looks at him incredulously.

Yeah, I kinda feel sorry for his ass, you know.

M'BALIA. *(Firmly.)* Don't. Your target is the oppressor. He is not a man, he is the enemy. He is the devil. The beast. Your target is zero. Compassion is an emotion that is wasted on him. When you eliminate your target, you are destroying a non-man. You are killing a no-thing. The oppressor's life is zero. The death of your target will mean life for the revolution. You should remember that. Reduce your enemy from humanity to zero. Once you have done that in your mind, such emotions as compassion cease to have relevancy, and pulling the trigger becomes easier and easier. Ultimately you can kill with the same nonchalance as brushing your hair.

KEUSI. You really believe that?

M'BALIA. Of course. I'm a revolutionary. The total extermination of the enemy is my goal. After you've been with us awhile, you'll come to adopt this point of view as well.

KEUSI. Yeah, uh-huh, well, I recognize my duty to fight and maybe die for the revolution, but I ain't never been able to see killin' in a machinelike fashion. I'm a man, not a machine.

M'BALIA. You refuse to understand. Compassion is beyond the emotional range of the true terrorist. We say that the only true emotion in the revolution is revolutionary fervor.

KEUSI. I can see that my education is going to be a long and hard one.

M'Balia looks at him but says nothing.

Hey, I'll tell you one thing, though: That info that Ahmed had on Savage was very meticulous. Whoever was assigned to check him out sure did a good job. Looks like they got his shit down pat.

M'BALIA. I watched the target. I worked as a maid in his house for a coupla months. I got to know him pretty well. He tried to get me to sleep with him a couple of times, but I kept refusing, so he fired me and got someone else. But by that time we had most of the information we needed. When I think about it, though, I should have slept with him. It would have been so easy to execute him then. One of the other sisters did it. I understand it works very well.

KEUSI. I don't see why y'all need a female assassins unit in the first place.

M'BALIA. Manpower needs dictated it. There just weren't enough brothers to do all that needed doing.

KEUSI. Yeah, but could you as a woman, a giver of life, teach a doctrine of terror and death to your children?

M'BALIA. I'll never know. I'm an assassin and we're not among those women who're allowed to have a husband and children. Our tasks are too dangerous and they require our full allegiance and dedication to what we do. Besides, our duty overshadows any considerations of love and/or motherhood.

KEUSI. But you will have a man and kids someday, won't you?

M'BALIA. I've devoted my life to the revolution. A man and children are luxuries a woman can afford when there's peace. We're at war and I haven't the time to even think of such things. And don't be getting any ideas. Just because I have a womb, don't think I'm that eager to put something in it. I won't be judged by my sex. I'm a revolutionary before I'm a woman.

> *Keusi and M'Balia look at each other. Keusi is bemused and M'Balia is dead serious. She starts out. A sly smile comes over Keusi's face.*

KEUSI. M'Balia?

> *She turns.*

Are you for real? Y'all really can take sex or leave it?

M'BALIA. *(Trying to deal with Keusi's insolence.)* Well…every now and then some of us still have the need, Keusi. After all, it is a natural human function, you know.

KEUSI. *(Smiling.)* Yes, I know.

M'BALIA. *(Insulted.)* Don't be vulgar.

KEUSI. M'Balia, you got a man?

M'BALIA. *(Bitingly.)* No. I haven't found one who interests me.

KEUSI. You sure?

> *Keusi looks at her. M'Balia avoids his eyes and the question.*

M'BALIA. I'll go clean your weapon. You should rest. You have important work to do.

KEUSI. Yeah, okay, *(Sarcastically.)* "Mommy."

> *Angry, M'Balia exits in a huff.*

Ain't this a bitch?

> *Keusi laughs to himself and lights up a joint. Lights go down.*

Scene 3

Lights up on Antar and Ahmed seated in the headquarters of the Black Terrorists.

ANTAR. You know, once we eliminate the oppressor Savage, we will have to be prepared for some very hectic times. Many of us will probably be killed.

AHMED. Yeah, I know. Well, we all have to die sometime. I guess going out with the blood of the oppressor on our hands is the best way for the true revolutionary to die.

ANTAR. Once Savage has been eliminated, we must prepare ourselves for full-scale reprisals. The oppressors will scour the entire Black community until they find us, and when they do, I guess it'll be a fight to the death.

AHMED. I know it'll be a fight to the death, 'cause I ain't hardly gonna go to jail behind destroying some oppressor.

ANTAR. Assassinating the oppressor will probably mean that another, more beastly oppressor will take his place. He will unleash the Night Rangers and that could signal the beginning of the next phase of the revolution: open all-out warfare between the Black community and the local forces of the oppressor. I just hope we are prepared.

AHMED. We're ready as ever. The Night Rangers will have one helluva time gettin' in here and if they do, they'll have less than half the men they started with, no matter how many men they send at us. The revolutionary example we set will inspire revolutionaries all over the world.

ANTAR. That's the greatest honor any revolutionary can have. The death cries of the enemy can serve as our dirge.

AHMED. Dig it.

ANTAR. It's good to know that, as a leader, I am surrounded by brothers of such courage. I know that none of you will let me down when the time comes.

AHMED. All of us except maybe that new brother.

ANTAR. Which one?

AHMED. Keusi Kifo.

ANTAR. What's the matter? Don't you trust him?

AHMED. I wouldn't go so far as to say that. But I am kinda worried about where his head is at.

ANTAR. You don't think he's the man, do you?

AHMED. No, we've had him followed and we've checked as thoroughly as we could on his background. He's clean as far as we can tell. Our spies in police headquarters said that they couldn't find nothin' on him, but they still keepin' they ears open. Kifo's a veteran of the Vietnam War and he's a weapons expert and was also a sniper. Much decorated and alla that shit. The brother who recommended him is one of our most trusted revolutionaries. No, I don't think he's the man. That's not the kind of vibration I get from him.

ANTAR. Well, then what's the trouble?

ARMED. I was with him a little while ago. He's a very incorrect brother. No discipline, no revolutionary fervor; just a very uncool nigger who acts as though what we're involved in is just an advanced stage of gang-banging.

ANTAR. I guess it's a carryover from his war experiences. You should remember that, unlike most of us, Kifo has fought and killed for a number of years while in Vietnam. This is all old hat to him. I think we should be patient and try to coax him along gently.

AHMED. Yeah, well, I went to check on his efficiency report an' that report ain't that good. I told you before that I didn't think he shoulda been selected for this mission. Just 'cause he got a good military record that don't mean that that's enough. Hey, man, listen to this report: "Too compassionate…given to feeling sorry for his targets… hangs on to such emotions as pity and mercy…doesn't realize that such emotions are beyond the range of the true revolutionary." Antar, any brother who got any kind of political knowledge knows that our situation in this country is the result of inhuman treatment that has in turn dehumanized us. We are outside humanity because inhuman beasts have forced us there. Now they threaten us because we seek to return to humanity. But the beast blocks our path. We got to use inhuman means to defeat inhumanity. See, Keusi Kifo won't acknowledge that fact and I feel that in the long run he gonna be a detriment to the organization.

ANTAR. I see. Ahmed, I think your suspicions have some validity, but on the other hand, the War Council decided unanimously on Ndugu Keusi, with you, of course, abstaining. It's too late to call everything off, now. The wheels of death for the oppressor are rolling and no one can stop them. My own opinion is that you exaggerate just a little. Kifo is certainly no troublemaker. Recognize that you've already decided that he is not the man and you've determined that he is a good killer. His loyalty, at this point, is not in doubt. So what you should understand, then, is that his lack of discipline and fervor are but the characteristics of a great many new members of this cadre. His fire is much like yours when you first came to us.

AHMED. But I understood the seriousness of what we did and what we had to do. Therefore I took the revolution seriously. I don't think Ndugu Keusi does and that's the shit that's botherin' me.

A young Terrorist bursts in, salutes, and addresses Antar.

YOUNG BROTHER. Excuse me, Mkuu Antar, but Geronimo of the American Liberation Front is outside. He's been shot in the shoulder and he's all beat-up lookin'.

ANTAR. How the hell... *(To the Young Brother.)* Bring him in here soon as you can.

YOUNG BROTHER. *(Saluting.)* Ndio, Mkuu Antar.

He exits in a hurry.

AHMED. Great, now Geronimo's ass is lit up. Who's gonna be next? We gonna have to put an end to this shit, man. Kifo better not fuck up. I'll put fire to his ass if he do.

ANTAR. *(Softly.)* Take it easy, man.

Two brothers bring in Geronimo. He is wearing a brightly colored headband, Apache-style moccasins laced up to his knees, and wears an army fatigue jacket. A sister, who remains silent and in the "background," enters and begins to dress Geronimo's wound.

SISTER. Please try to relax, my brother. This is going to hurt a bit.

GERONIMO. *(Ignoring the sister; to no one in particular.)* Those white motherfuckers!! Goddamn spiritless, devil-eyed dogs! Aw, man! Oh man!! Goddamn!!!

ANTAR. *(Calmly.)* Geronimo, be cool. Calm down.

GERONIMO. The pigs, man, the pigs!!! They put all my best shit to sleep!

AHMED. Geronimo, damn, man, make some sense.

GERONIMO. The Night Rangers destroyed my headquarters, man. They took weapons, records, smoke, everything. Three of my men are dead, more of my warriors are wounded or in hiding, and I'm here all shot up.

SISTER. Geronimo, I'll have to ask you not to move so much. I can't fix your bandages right if you keep movin' like you do.

GERONIMO. *(Ignoring the request.)* The bullet went clean through my shoulder, man. I ain't never been shot before. It hurt like hell, but it was wild. Ow! Goddamn, watch it, sister!

SISTER. I'm sorry, my brother, but I told you before it was gonna hurt.

GERONIMO. Yeah, well, okay, sister. But don't let it hurt too much.

AHMED. You gonna tell us what happened, man?

GERONIMO. Yeah, okay. This was extremely well planned and coordinated. They killed Ramon, my Chief of Security; Victor, my Chief of Culture; and Juney-bugs, my Chief of Propaganda. I think the Night Rangers probably got all my records. If they do then they got the who's who of every chapter in the country. They got a list of all my known contacts and a list of the white boys who was payin' my expenses when I gave speeches at colleges and shit like that. Man, the pigs got the American Liberation Front by the balls.

AHMED. I guess y'all have had it, brother. You better make preparations to go underground and split.

GERONIMO. Hell no! That punk Commissioner Savage pulled off this shit and I want his ass! He's responsible for the deaths of three of the baddest brothers who ever lived. I shaped and molded those cats myself. Victor, Ramon, and Juney-bugs was smokers, man; very righteous revolutionaries. Good sharp minds. They learned well and followed orders to the letter. Damn, man, they was *revolutionaries*! Man, I shudda died with them. They were the best, man. You know?

ANTAR. You still haven't told us what's happened.

GERONIMO. *(Angry; excited.)* Hey, man! Goddamn! I told you, the pigs vamped on us!

AHMED. How? I thought y'all had some security.

GERONIMO. We figured we did. We had these five Marxist white boys covering for us.

AHMED. White boys?! Aw, *man*!! Geronimo, was you crazy?!

GERONIMO. Well, hey, man, we thought they was different.

AHMED. See, man, we told you about that alliance shit in the first place.

GERONIMO. We thought they was bad, man. You know, these cats been blowin' up the Bank of America, draft offices, Dupont Chemical property, goin' on days of rage and shit, and quotin' Marx better than the Russians. You know, these cats was those crazy motherfuckers who called themselves "The Narodnikis." Hey, man, we thought we had some dynamite dudes with us…and the pink pussies punked out!!! The pigs musta moved fast 'cause the first thing we knew Finkel and Schmidt came bustin' thru the door headin' for the escape tunnel shouting, "Pigs outside! Pigs outside! Let's get the hell outta here!" They hit the tunnel shaft and we didn't see them no more.

ANTAR. We told you a long time ago about alliances with those white radicals. They are either suicidal in outlook or thrill-seekers who have no real stomach for true revolution. I thought that a lesson had been learned by all of you alliance-prone brothers after the way Bobby got used in Chicago a couple of years ago.

AHMED. The only place for white boys in the struggle is *outside* the struggle.

GERONIMO. Yeah, I realize that, now. They all the same, all those white radicals. All they can do is sell woof tickets and hide behind Black revolutionaries' coattails, waitin' for us to tell them what to do next. They stand around wavin' Viet Cong flags and shit, and spittin' at pigs. But soon as they start gettin' they heads cracked by some pigs, they start cryin' and shouting. (*Very effeminate.*) "Oh my God, what's happening. But we're the kids! We're the kids!" They got no heart, man. No heart at all. They don't understand revolution. Not really. So fuck 'em! They all pussies! The faggots, they oughta drop they pants and spread they "cheeks." That's all they good for, anyway.

> *Geronimo calms down a bit. Tries to pull himself together.*

SISTER. Brother, you gonna have to try to control yourself. I can't do nothin' for your shoulder if you remain in your overexcited state.

GERONIMO. (*Breathing hard; looks at the sister a moment. Face grows hard.*) Aw, later for my shoulder. My men lyin' dead, wounded, and scattered all over the fuckin' city. And you botherin' me about a stupid-ass flesh wound! Fuck my shoulder. Woman, get away from me, I ain't asked you for your advice!!

> *Hurt, the Sister quietly bows her head and starts to leave. Ahmed looks hard at Geronimo, who does not notice him. He seems almost in another world. Realizing he has been rash, Geronimo takes the sister's arm.*

Wait, hold it, sister. Please stay. I'm sorry. You doin' a good job. Please...I'm sorry.

> *Geronimo kisses the sister on the cheek.*

Finish what you were doin'. I'll try to be cool.

> *The sister looks at Antar, who nods approvingly; she smiles slightly at Geronimo and resumes dressing his wound. It takes only a few seconds and she has finished. Having done that, she moves to a quiet corner of the room, where she remains.*

That's a good job, my sister. You do your work well.

SISTER. Asante, Ndugu Geronimo.

GERONIMO. (*Smiles.*) Hey, man, that's a beautiful sister. I almost forget what I been through when I look at her. You know?

> *The sister smiles.*

But I can't forget. Nothin' can ever make me forget. Nothin'll make me forget what went when those pigs staged they massacre. But we made them pay. We made them pay!

> *Geronimo becomes exhilarated as he relates the following details.*

Me, Ramon, and three other brothers was on the windows. Juney-bugs was downstairs guardin' the door. Everybody else scattered at every other available position. We put the steel shutters up. Then I put a sister on the phone callin' up the Black radio station, so she could tell the shit as it was happenin'. I didn't want the pigs floodin' the airwaves with their version of battle. We had to be ready for those motherfuckers on every level. These pigs was the Night Rangers an' we knew they was better armed than the 101st Airborne, so we wasn't takin' no chances. Then these two pigs tried to dynamite the door open. Ramon leaned out the window an' fired twice: Bam! Bam! Two pigs fell for the revolution! AAAAAAAAIIIIIIIEEEEEEE!!!!!! Then, I heard a loud crunch an' I saw Ramon's face turn into a charred lump of blood. Ramon! Ramon! Oh man, goddamn... But we held 'em, man. The chumps threw everything they could at us an' we held 'em off. Then there was an explosion an' screams an' the place was fillin' up with smoke. They finally managed to dynamite the door open. The explosion busted Juney-bugs all up. He couldn't move, man. The brother didn't have a chance. But that didn't stop Juney-bugs. He had a piece in each hand. The first four pigs thru the door died. Juney was settin' a beautiful revolutionary example: four pigs lyin' dead at his feet, two more lyin' wounded in the door-way cryin' for they mamas an' they gods. Juney-bugs just kept on firin' into that cloud of smoke an' not one pig dared to move from behind the cars an' shit they was hidin' behind. An', man, there was bullets zingin' all past my head, people screamin', guns an' shit, an' I was feelin'...I was feelin'...damn about nothin'. I could feel the spirits of all the great revolutionaries with me. Man, it was like I was feelin' mystical an' shit. An' then, with everything blowin' up all around me, I saw the spirit of death laughin' at me. He raised a clenched fist. An' I raised a clenched fist an' shouted, "Right on, motherfucker!!!" an' laughed back. I swear to God, man, an' I'm ashamed to admit it, but I loved it! I LOVED IT! We was heavin' the righteous wrath of the people on the pigs. *(Hysterical laugher.)* HAH AHAHAHAHAHAHAHAHAHAHAHAHAHAHAHAHAHA!!!!! Another explosion an' there was only seven of us left alive by this time. I could hear the pigs comin' up the stairs an' I knew that Juney-bugs musta been killed. It was time to get outta there. We got the sistuhs out first... Then, man, the craziest thing: Victor knelt down beside

Ramon's body an' he put his hand in his blood, an' he started tremblin' an' screamin' an' actin' wild an' shit. He charged the pigs, firin' as he went. No! No! Nooooooo!!!… It was just me, now. I ran inside the main room an' bolted the door shut. I could hear the pigs tryin' to bust it down. I set the room on fire. Couldn't afford to let the pigs get nothin'. Then someone shot thru the door an' I got hit. I started to fall, but I held on. I knew if the pigs found me alive, they'd kill me on the spot. I started to crawl to the tunnel. The room was burnin' when I left, but I'm sure the devils musta been able to put the fire out an' get those files.

AHMED. You shudda had summa those sisters destroyin' those files the minute the first shot was fired.

GERONIMO. They was all upstairs on the third floor when the shit started. An' they was asleep. When the shit started, it was started. Either you shot or got shot. There was not time to worry about files.

ANTAR. You should have taken time, Geronimo. Now, the whole Front's gotta go underground or maybe even disband. The FBI's gonna be bustin' ass right and left.

GERONIMO. My only hope is that the fire I set took care of business. That's all I got to say on the matter, so don't be bustin' my ass about no goddamn files.

    His mood changes. Body sags a bit.

Oh, man, those three brothers. Oh, man, they was so beautiful. Blazin' away even as they fell. Ramon, with his face blown off, lay on the floor still holdin' his piece. Even in death he was settin' a perfect revolutionary example. Man, why do dynamite brothers like those three cats always have to be the ones to get offed?

ANTAR. They have attained the ultimate freedom in this oppressive condition Black people live in, Geronimo. Those brothers chose to die rather than live in squalor and deprivation. Their concern for their plight and the plight of their Black brothers and sisters all over the world led them to sacrifice the ultimate for a remedy to their situation. Those of us who are left can only be inspired by their revolutionary deaths.

AHMED. That's right, my brother. Even in death the brothers have provided impetus for the revolution.

During the last exchange the sister has moved to Geronimo's side to inspect his bandages.

SISTER. Mkuu Geronimo, you movin' so much you startin' to bleed again.

GERONIMO. *(Looking at the wound.)* Wow. Dig that.

He touches the wound, then pulls his hand away, marveling at the sight of the blood. Then, he clenches his fist and closes his eyes.

Oh man, oh man! I can feel it, my brothers! The revolution, Victor, Juney-bugs, and Ramon. I can feel it all. Oh, my God!

The sister tries to re-dress his wound, but he pushes her hand away.

No don't!! Not yet.

He places his hand over the wound once more.

Yeah…yeah… Now, I know what Victor felt when he touched Ramon's blood. My wrist! Alla y'all grab aholda my wrist.

He clenches his fist. All grab his wrist.

Can you feel it? You feel the spirits? You feel 'em? Oh God, it's beautiful. Can you feel it, brothers? Can you feel it, sister? It's the spirit of the revolution. Can't nothin' hurt me, now; I know it!! Oh, wow, man! The blood! The feeling! It's really taking me out.

SISTER. Geronimo, you're trembling all over.

AHMED. He must be getting' the fever.

GERONIMO. *(Angry.)* It ain't no goddamn fever!! It's the revolution. It's my only reason for being alive from this moment on! To fight and die for the revolution. I won't live beyond it! I don't want to. I don't care what goes down after we win. I only want to live to destroy my enemy. Once that has been, my usefulness to the revolution will be done. From now on, I'm a revolutionary warrior. I live for the battle. Peace would kill me. I only want to live to destroy my enemy. That's my goal. Death and destruction will be my weapons of war. *(Clenching his fist tighter.)* Oh God, can y'all feel it? The blood is burning in my fist.

ANTAR. *(Looks warily at the others.)* Geronimo, maybe you'd better try and rest. You keep up like this and you'll lose a lot of blood and that could lead to you dyin'.

GERONIMO. No, man, not! Not Geronimo! Geronimo ain't gonna die on no hummer. I seen my death. I'm gonna die like a revolutionary with the blood of the enemy on my hands. To die for the revolution is a glorious thing. It is, man, it is. Make no mistake. I'll meet my moment in a true revolutionary manner.

My brothers, I ain't splittin' into no goddamn exile. I'm stayin' here to fight and die in the revolution. Let me join you. I need to hook up with some revolutionary freedom fighters. Let me work with you. Please. Y'all are revolutionaries, an' I'm one, too. Don't deny me the chance to get even for Victor, Ramon, and Juney-bugs.

ANTAR. *(Smiling.)* Geronimo, you were always one of us, my brother. We would be honored to have you serve with us.

    They embrace.

AHMED. Death to the oppressors!!

ANTAR. Long life to the revolution!!!

GERONIMO. Death and destruction! Pain and agony! Let the blood of the enemy flow in the streets purifying the revolutionary cause. Let nothing remain standing before the power for the revolution!!!

ALL. AAAAAAIIIIIIIIEEEEEEE!!!!!!!!!!!!!

    Blackness.

Scene 4

    A few days later in the apartment occupied by Keusi and M'Balia. He and M'Balia are eating. The radio blares in the background.

RADIO NEWSMAN. …And now the top news story of the week: Some eighty-five policemen, members of the elite Night Rangers, earlier this week raided the headquarters of the American Liberation Front at 221 Chapel Street in the Penny Lane District. Twenty-two persons, including thirteen policemen, were killed in the blazing twenty-minute gun battle that ensued when police reported that they were met with gunfire when they sought entrance to the headquarters to ask the ownership of a Volkswagen double-parked illegally outside.

Police eventually had to use a special cannon and dynamite to gain entrance to the building, which was destroyed by fire in a successful attempt to destroy certain records and files that the ALF members apparently did not want the police to obtain. The bodies of nine members of the ALF, seven males and two females, were found in the rubble. Police have also had to deal with increasing sniping incidents in the surrounding neighborhood, as well as with rampaging bands of Black youths who have been attacking foot patrolmen from rooftops.

Now, as we had promised earlier, here is a tape of the telephone call the WORL newsroom received from the ALF headquarters during the height of the gun battle that has been declared the bloodiest in the annals of modern American law enforcement:

> *We hear the sound of a woman's voice amid the reports of gunfire and explosions, shouts and screams.*

REVOLUTIONARY SISTER. …The revolutionary headquarters of the American Liberation Front are now under siege from the racist, fascist, reactionary army of the pig power structure. They are attacking us with everything but we are holding firm. Already, at least three pigs have been barbecued, with minimal losses to ourselves.

> *Explosion. Screams. Voice more excited.*

Now the pigs look like they usin' cannon, but we still holdin' on. The revolution is moving to a higher level. Right on! Death to the fascist dogs and the imperialist criminals who control them! Death to the enemies of the lumpenproletariat! Long live the revolution!!

> *More shots, screams, more explosions.*

They throwin' everything at us, yet we will persevere because we must!…

> *Tape is abruptly cut. The Newsman takes over.*

RADIO NEWSMAN. That was the voice of one of the members of the American Liberation Front speaking to this office in the midst of the shootout with the Night Rangers that took the lives…

> *M'Balia rises from the table and cuts off the radio.*

M'BALIA. Yessir! The American Liberation Front stone took care of business.

KEUSI. *(Nonchalantly.)* Yeah.

M'BALIA. They really did the job, man. I bet the oppressors never expected to be met with such revolutionary fervor. Thirteen oppressors revolutionized to death.

KEUSI. At the cost of the lives of nine ALF warriors. Alla that death and gunplay was unnecessary, if you can dig it.

M'BALIA. Unnecessary? Their deaths had meaning. They died in order that the revolution might carry on. In that respect, their deaths were necessary.

KEUSI. You know you got too much idealism. That's your problem. You gotta recognize that at this stage, the death of *any* revolutionary is needless. We haven't the strength to face the honky on a large scale, yet. We can't even keep pushers outta our neighborhood with any real success, so how can we run down a program of armed struggle against the beast? Hit-and-run tactics, at best, are all we can do. The ALF had an out and didn't use it.

M'BALIA. They had no out. They had to fight. They had no choice other than to fight and die like men, or surrender and be herded to the electric chair in shackles. Those brothers and sisters chose to commit revolutionary suicide and in doing so advanced the revolution even farther. There is no tragedy in their deaths; only glory.

KEUSI. Hey, baby, how you gonna talk about glorious death, when to get killed now is really not necessary?

M'BALIA. In our daily struggles against the oppressor, the possibility of death is always present, no matter what level the revolution is being waged on. We acknowledge death and do not fear it.

KEUSI. But the revolution is about life—I thought. Our first duty as revolutionaries is to live.

M'BALIA. Is it? The first duty of the true revolutionary is to kill the oppressor and destroy his works.

KEUSI. But don't that come when the revolutionaries have got strength? Until that time he got to live, and he can't do that practicing revolutionary suicide.

M'BALIA. *(Angry.)* And when the tables are turned against him, when every avenue is blocked, every alternative closed to him, what then must the revolutionary do? *(Without waiting for answer.)* He must fight! He must fight or die. He has no choice. When his back is to the wall, he can't die like a lamb waiting the slaughter. No, let him have his gun and his manhood.

KEUSI. *(Silent a moment.)* Yeah, okay, my sister. But I still think Geronimo was crazy to pursue a gun battle with the police. See, like, his back wasn't totally to the wall. What he did was cause his headquarters to get burned down, nine brothers and sisters to lose their lives, and for the revolution to suffer another bad day.

M'BALIA. How can you say that?

KEUSI. 'Cause from listening to the reports and from having known some brothers who belonged to that chapter of the ALF, I know that the gunfight wasn't necessary.

M'BALIA. Are you accusing him of being a traitor?

KEUSI. No. I'm accusin' him of piss-poor leadership.

M'BALIA. What the hell do you know about it?! Who are you to say something like that?

KEUSI. I can't say what I want?

M'BALIA. Not when you go around disparaging one of the baddest brothers walkin'. I think you should watch your mouth. Ahmed is right. One of these days you're gonna be stepped on.

KEUSI. I guess I'll have to worry about that when the time comes, 'cause when I see things I feel are goin' wrong I gotta speak out. I've seen some things in the past week that have got me wonderin' what's happenin'. Suddenly, you know, I'm like, questioning which way the revolution is going.

M'BALIA. You're just afraid of revolution. That's what it is. You're afraid of a real revolution.

KEUSI. Damn right, if people like Geronimo are gonna be leadin' it. All the revolutionaries I've seen ever since I came outta the indoctrination classes got a colossal death wish. We all bein' oriented toward death. Once you get hooked goin' that way, everything you do is geared toward destruction and finally you can't think positively or constructively.

M'BALIA. Oh, I can think positive, alright. The most positive thing

I can think of is the death of the oppressor. Ahmed once said that we shall bathe in the oppressor's blood on the day of our victory.

KEUSI. Suppose I was to say that we could build the Black nation without even firing a shot, if we really wanted to do that?

M'BALIA. I'd call you an insufferable romantic fool and a threat to the revolutionary fervor we are trying to promote in the people.

KEUSI. Yeah, M'Balia, I can see why Antar has placed you with me. I'm sure gonna learn a lot from you.

M'BALIA. You need to. You lack all kinds of revolutionary zeal.

KEUSI. Baby, I'm a trained killer. I've seen shit that would have you vomitin' all over this place and I seen buddies of mine die right in my arms. So what the hell're you talkin' about? Zeal? What the hell is some goddamn zeal? Zeal don't mean shit when it comes down to it. What counts then is quick thinking, discipline, holdin' up under pressure, and common sense. Zeal will get you killed if you don't watch out.

M'BALIA. Your incorrect mouth may get *you* killed.

> *M'Balia rises without further comment and begins moving about the apartment straightening up. Her movements are graceful and very feminine. This is brought about by the lapa she wears. Keusi lights a cigarette and watches her awhile, a wry and gentle smile coming over his face.*

KEUSI. Hey, baby, tell me somethin'. When's the last time you been treated like a woman.

M'BALIA. I don't know what you're talking about. I'm always treated like a woman.

KEUSI. Well, Antar said that you was to be my wife and do everything a man expects of a woman.

M'BALIA. Provided I'm in the mood. Now look, I told you about this once before. Don't be disrespectful.

KEUSI. I'm not being disrespectful. I'm being a man.

M'BALIA. Well, I don't think I want you to make love to me.

KEUSI. A fine-lookin' sister like you? I'm sure you must need *some* lovin' *some*time.

M'BALIA. I'm—a Black Terrorist. Sex isn't a thing with me anymore.

34

Keusi bursts into a great laugh.

Well, what's so funny?

KEUSI. *(Laughing.)* Yeah, okay, baby, we all must make sacrifices for the revolution.

He laughs harder.

M'BALIA. You stop laughing at me! There's nothing funny. It's the truth. A true revolutionary has no time for such emotions. I'm a Black Terrorist…

KEUSI. *(Interrupting.)* You're a woman…

M'BALIA. I'm an expert assassin…

KEUSI. You're supposed to get fucked and have babies. Let the men fight.

M'BALIA. That's not true. The Black Terrorist Women's Organization said that my main function was that of a revolutionary, not those mundane feminine things. I'm a free woman, not a whore.

KEUSI. Aw, woman, ain't nobody said you wasn't a revolutionary. Now, c'mere and shut up!!

Keusi moves toward her.

M'BALIA. *(Backing away.)* Keep away from me.

She strikes a karate stance.

You keep away from me, you hear!

> *Keusi moves on her, whereupon she tosses his behind on the floor. Keusi looks up at her in angered bewilderment. He rises slowly and faces her. Gradually he begins to relax, then smiles. Eventually, M'Balia, feeling she has made her point, lets her guard down. At that instant Keusi smacks the shit outta her. She hits the ground hard on her behind. She fights back a few tears. Keusi kneels beside her.*

KEUSI. Awww, what's these? Revolutionary tears? I thought you was beyond such emotion.

> *He laughs, reaches into pocket, and wipes her tears away with a handkerchief.*

You're a woman before anything else. When I get through with you, you'll never want to forget that. Now, come here and don't hand me

35

nunna that "I'm a revolutionary" bullshit.

He pulls her close.

Hey, baby, you lookin' g-o-o-o-o-d.

Keusi begins to undress her as the lights go down.

Lights up on Keusi and M'Balia lying together.

Hey, baby, I'm sorry I hit you.

M'BALIA. You could have broken my jaw.

KEUSI. Aw, the only thing hurt was your pride. I half pushed you, anyway. I'm sorry, though, honest.

She does not answer him.

Hey, baby, I really mean it.

Keusi leans over and kisses M'Balia long and hard.

See?

M'BALIA. Yes. I believe you, but…well, Keusi, you know this can't lead to anything. I can't get involved with you in any deep way because I'm an assassin and because of what I do. I won't always be able to see you. Let's end it, now. We had a good little time, but—

KEUSI. Uh-uh. We ain't endin' nothin'. I dug you the first time I laid eyes on you an' I ain't gonna lose you now.

M'BALIA. Keusi, my life belongs to the revolution. I live it and breathe it. Anything beyond that just isn't real for me. To become your woman, I'd have to leave the Female Assassins unit, and I could never do that. I've been with them for two and a half years; I've lived with them, and laughed and cried with them. They're my family, my sisters in the revolution. I just can't up and leave them.

KEUSI. Yes, you can.

M'BALIA. No. It's impossible. *(Hoping to change the subject.)* Hey, you'd better get some sleep. Tomorrow's the day you eliminate the oppressor.

KEUSI. *(Smiling.)* Sleep is somethin' I don't wanna do, right now. *(Half-whisper.)* Now, c'mere.

He kisses M'Balia as the lights go down.

Scene 5

Lights up. The next day—very late...evening. M'Balia worriedly paces the floor, Keusi appears in the doorway. He carries a duffle bag with him, his appearance grim. M'Balia stands in frozen expectation, watching him. Keusi slowly nods his head. Excitedly, M'Balia approaches him.

M'BALIA. There's no doubt? He's dead?

KEUSI. *(Quietly.)* They should find his body in his driveway a coupla hours from now. Maybe sooner.

> *M'Balia embraces him. Keusi gently pushes her away. Reaches into his pocket and takes out a slip of paper and pencil. He writes a telephone number down.*

Here, call this number. Let the phone ring three times. Then hang up. That'll signal success.

> *M'Balia does as she is told. Keusi moves into room and sits wearily. He removes his shoes and begins to unwind. M'Balia finishes the telephone call, then approaches Keusi.*

M'BALIA. *(Looking at duffle bag with curiosity.)* How...how did you do it? I got worried when I looked into the room and saw you didn't take any of your weapons.

> *As she rummages thru the bag she comes up with a crossbow and takes it out of the bag. Keusi sits quietly, not really paying any attention. M'Balia eyes it, both repulsed and fascinated at the same time.*

Keusi, did you use this?

KEUSI. *(Remembering every detail of the assassination.)* Yeah...it was simple.

> *He laughs sardonically, then becomes silent again. Noticing M'Balia with the crossbow, Keusi takes it from her and puts it back in duffle bag.*

(Tired and drawn.) Yeah...so simple.

M'BALIA. Did anyone spot you?

KEUSI. No.

M'BALIA. But a crossbow? I don't understand.

KEUSI. Quick, silent, and very accurate.

M'BALIA. That's all you got to say?

KEUSI. What else is there to say?

M'BALIA. I suppose you're right. Um…are you hungry?

> *Keusi looks at her, then looks away.*

Is there…is there anything I can do?

> *Keusi lies down. M'Balia gets some oils, moves to him, and begins massaging Keusi's back.*

KEUSI. Oh, baby…I'm tired. So goddamn tired.

M'BALIA. *(Massaging.)* This will help you relax.

KEUSI. He looked right at me…right at me… I saw him get out of his car. I took aim an' I fired. The arrow hit him in the back of the neck. He turned around and he had this weird, twisted, and frightened look on his face. He saw me…he reached out, and started staggering toward me, bleedin' and coughin' blood… Then he fell dead. But his eyes was open, lookin' right at me… Right at me.

> *With suddenness Keusi takes M'Balia in his arms.*

Baby…baby…baby. Lemme just hold you.

> *He holds her tight.*

God, it's so good to be alive. Living, breathing, loving. Never aware it can end on a hummer in a minute. Baby, lemme just hold you an' be glad I'm alive…

> *They embrace and kiss as lights go down.*

Scene 6

The headquarters of the Black Terrorists. Antar, Ahmed, and Geronimo are seated together. Laid out before them is what appears to be a large diagram. Also, an assortment of maps are strewn about.

GERONIMO. There, that's it. Whatch'all think? We can plant bombs under the sewers *(Pointing to diagram.)* along here. And here. You see? When they blow, those streets will be rendered useless. Also, looka here. *(Reaching for another diagram.)* This one's of the police station itself and shows that we can plant another bomb here and disrupt their whole communications thing. We can drop charges in other places. Look, me, Juney-bugs, Ramon, and Victor went over these plans backwards and forwards, in and out, day and night.

ANTAR. I don't know, Geronimo. I'm hesitant to try something like that.

GERONIMO. Me and my three chiefs went over this thing for months, man. It can work. Why you against it?

ANTAR. It's risky, man. It doesn't sound all that foolproof. I'm not all that sure it can work.

GERONIMO. You tryin' to say somethin'?

ANTAR. No, Geronimo—

GERONIMO. Don't be disparaging the memory of those three young brothers. They had good minds, man. They don't put together no shoddy shit.

ANTAR. I'm well aware of that. But I still feel that it's too risky. How do we know that the oppressors won't be guarding against just such a maneuver?

GERONIMO. *(Annoyed.)* The whole goddamn revolution is risky, Antar. Any revolutionary move you make involves the element of risk. What the hell you rappin' about?

AHMED. *(To Antar.)* I think it's a good idea, Antar. Psychologically, it'll blow the Man's mind.

ANTAR. I don't know. That kind of terrorism involves high risk.

We've usually operated against lesser targets and much closer to home. I think more planning is needed. We have to look into every angle.

GERONIMO. What's there to look at? We have a target, we destroy it. No bullshit, no questions; destroy the target. Hey, man, you brothers terrorists or not?

ANTAR. *(Calmly.)* We're terrorists.

GERONIMO. Then what the fuck's the problem?

ANTAR. That kind of guerrilla tactic is the problem. It may be beyond our particular training. I think we should be more cautious.

GERONIMO. Motherfuck, caution!!

> *Ahmed looks angrily at Geronimo, but Antar restrains him with a silent gesture.*

Hey, man, look! All you do is get in the goddamn sewers, crawl through 'em, plant the bombs, and split. The men be underground. Who the fuck's gonna spot them?!

ANTAR. *(Calmly.)* Listen. Your idea is a good one. But I'm only trying to say that the nature of the venture requires more careful planning. Yes, I could give you some of my men, but they will run the risk of being detected in an action against a target all the way across town from the nearest Black neighborhood. If they are discovered, they can be trapped in those sewers and slaughtered like animals. All you've done is show me some diagrams, blue-prints. Juney-bugs was the only one of the three of you who had ever been in that jail before, and that was only for a brief stay. He couldn't have possibly gotten the most precise information needed for an operation of this sort. Add to that the possibility of those diagrams y'all stole being old as anything and we could really have problems. Suppose the oppressors have renovated those buildings? We wouldn't even know it. And tell me, have you been in those sewers out there? Have you studied the logistics of getting men— *Black* men and bombs undetected into a white neighborhood that is already cringing in fear because of our activities? You know as well as I do that that area is heavily patrolled by the police. Have you taken that into account. My brother—

GERONIMO. *(Hurt; interrupting.)* Man, why you trying to stop this plan?

ANTAR. I'm not trying to stop the plan. I actually tend to agree with Ahmed. It would be a major psychological blow to the oppressor. But I want a more carefully laid out plan. I'd like to see all my people get back safely.

GERONIMO. Yeah, well, okay, Mkuu Antar. But you should recognize the inevitability of revolutionary death.

ANTAR. I do. But I don't want all my revolutionaries dying at once.

AHMED. I like the idea, Antar. If it's the implementation of it that worries you then I'd like to volunteer to work with Geronimo on a new plan that will meet with your approval. *(To Geronimo.)* Provided that's all right with you, brother.

GERONIMO. I'd be very proud, Ahmed. I've always had the highest respect for you. So did Victor, Ramon, and Juney-bugs.

> *Just then, sounds of squeals of delight, shouts, and pandemonium are heard. A brother enters with a wide smile on his face. He snaps smartly to attention, salutes.*

BROTHER. Antar! I am pleased to report to you that Ndugu Keusi Kifo has eliminated Commissioner Savage. The brother has offed the pig!! Keusi Kifo has offed the pig!!

AHMED. Wooooeeeeeeee!!!

> *Joyous laughing.*

GERONIMO. *(At first unbelieving.)* The motherfucker's dead?! He's dead?!

> *The brother nods.*

AAAAIIIEEEE!!!! He's dead! The beast is dead! His blood shall feed the revolution!!! Victor, Ramon, Juney-bugs! The motherfucker is dead! AAAIIIEEEEE!!!!

ANTAR. *(As others enter; amid the shouts.)* This is the greatest moment in our brief history. The most brutal of all oppressors outside the federal government has been successfully eliminated. His death has opened the floodgates. The very foundations on which the oppressive law and order machine of this country is built is now quaking. But we can't stop here. The revolution must continue. More oppressors must die! There must be more victories! More life! More life for our parents, our brothers and sisters. More life for generations of Black people to come. Death to the oppressors! We shall be victorious.

Cheers.

AHMED. We are the Black Terrorists, sworn to the liberation of our people!

ALL. May we never lose sight of our duty!

AHMED. We seek the death of those who oppress us!

ALL. May our vengeance be as swift as lightning! AAAAIIIIEEEE!!!

More celebration. After a while, Keusi and M'Balia enter amid cheers and congratulatory remarks. He moves to Antar, salutes him, and is embraced by Antar, Ahmed, and Geronimo. M'Balia receives the same greeting, then is whisked off by the women. Cheering continues as lights dim to denote passage of time. Lights up on the aftermath of the celebration. Enter a sister with refreshments and places them before Keusi, Ahmed, M'Balia, Antar, and Geronimo, who are seated in that order. The sister exits.

ANTAR. A job well done, Ndugu Keusi. Zaidi ya asante.

Keusi smiles.

But we gathered here not only to express our thanks. We have another assignment for you.

KEUSI. *(Surprised.)* Wow, I just…

ANTAR. We know, but this man is even more dangerous than Savage.

GERONIMO. *(Excited; interrupting.)* Whatchu use on the beast, man?

KEUSI. A crossbow.

GERONIMO. *(Laughing.)* Oh, wow! A crossbow? Check the cat out for gettin' into some Robin Hood.

All laugh except for Keusi.

KEUSI. *(As if trying to provoke something.)* That's historically incorrect, Ndugu Geronimo.

GERONIMO. Huh?

KEUSI. I said you're wrong. Your reference is historically incorrect. The crossbow came after Robin Hood.

GERONIMO. Oh, I didn't know.

42

KEUSI. A lotta things you don't know, Geronimo.

The two men stare at each other. M'Balia attempts to intercede.

M'BALIA. Antar, any new information on Radcliffe?

KEUSI. That's my new target?

M'Balia nods and Keusi's face grows solemn. He appears worried.

ANTAR. Nothing beyond the information you supplied us with some time ago, M'Balia.

AHMED. Keusi, when you gonna get started on Radcliffe? That nigger's gotta go.

KEUSI. *(Quietly.)* I guess I'll start first thing tomorrow. Anything special about him I oughta know?

M'BALIA. Nothing really. His son is dead, and his wife died of a heart attack years ago.

KEUSI. What happen, his son get killed in Nam, or something?

GERONIMO. Hell no, he died fighting the enemy right here in the mother country.

M'BALIA. He died in a raid on a Panther headquarters two years ago. He was the only Panther to die. To show you what a lackey Radcliffe is, he refused to let any Panthers attend the funeral and swore to destroy Black militants because he said they had destroyed his son.

KEUSI. He must have loved his son a lot to be feelin' like that.

M'BALIA. That's beside the point. Radcliffe is an oppressor. He must die.

KEUSI. No doubt. But actually, to tell you the truth, I hate to be the one to set the precedent for killing our own people. Fratricide oughta always be avoided 'cause it's the one kinda killin' that always gets outta hand. Look at Biafra and Nigeria. The death is appalling. Ain't there no other way to handle this misguided cat?

GERONIMO. No. He dies. Don't try to rationalize a way for this ass-licking scab to live. Off him!!

M'BALIA. He has sworn to destroy us, Keusi. It's almost an obsession with him. You heard him on that news broadcast when he turned three of our brothers in to the oppressors.

Lights go out. Stage black. Spot picks up on Chauncey Radcliffe standing on a remote part of the stage.

RADCLIFFE. It's time the decent, law-abiding Negro citizens of this country stood up and shouted "Enough!" It's time for us to bring to an end this lunacy, this—this madness being perpetrated on our society today. We are fed up with being identified with these young fools. They are trying to tear down the greatest country in the world. America may have her faults, but there is no place on earth where the Negro has it this good. We're better off today than at any time in our history. We go to better schools, we have better jobs—better housing. Our middle class is growing stronger every day. What right do these disgruntled young thugs—for that's just what they are—thugs—what right have they to trample upon the rights and land for which so many Americans, colored and white, have died. These young disgruntles—spoiled brats and hooligans— are the creation of the television age. The sensationalist news media ignore the legitimate Negro leaders who are making positive contributions to Negro progress. They ignore those of us in my generation who've toiled for years, battling against mindless white racists on the one hand and Black fanatics on the other. Quiet but steady progress can't fit into the late news, so the media cover the misinformed Black-Power boys. Why? Because they make sensational news copy.

Well, I tell you, such madness has to stop. The responsible Negro element, the only true voice of the Negro since he first set foot on these shores; the responsible Negro element, which has survived the likes of Paul Cuffe, David Walker, Martin Delaney, Garvey, and the brilliant but misguided Malcolm X, now declares war on these young thugs. We will assist all local, state, and federal authorities in whatever way we can, in bringing to justice these criminals. They terrorize Negro communities and drive away our white friends who have suffered many humiliations while still standing at our sides. The three boys I have turned in today were only the beginning. By working with my good friend Commissioner Charles Savage, I solemnly swear to you that all of the revolutionaries, Black or white, Jew or Gentile, will be brought to justice.

Lights down. Lights up on the headquarters.

KEUSI. Yeah, sister. I guess you're right.

GERONIMO. When the French people staged the French Revolution, a lotta French heads rolled. When the Anarchists tried to rip off Paris in the 1850s, more Frenchmen died. When the Bolsheviks changed the course of world history in Russia, they offed thousands of fellow Russians, and so on down the line, brother. When Mao took China, the blood of fellow Chinamen flowed like a mighty river. Before we can move on the enemy without, we gotta move on the enemy within. Killing the arch-traitor Radcliffe is necessary.

KEUSI. With you killing is always necessary.

AHMED. Look, man, we don't like the idea any more than you do, but the nigger's crimes can't be ignored. He cursed the name of the Panthers and assisted in the destruction of their headquarters, he turned in three of our men, and he drove his only daughter from his household when she refused to support his schemes. This lap dog seeks our deaths, man. What else we supposed to do?

M'BALIA. The faggot lackey is a scar on the face of the Black community. He must die.

GERONIMO. A pig is a pig is a pig, be he Black or white. When he oinks, his breath still stinks.

ANTAR. Ndugu Keusi, you must recognize that we have no other choice. To allow him to live is to invite our own deaths. Sooner or later the police may succeed in making one of those three prisoners talk and give away the location of this headquarters. A lot of blood's gonna flow. We have sworn it. And all of that will come about because of this man's treachery. Radcliffe is an oppressor—with the oppressor's values, the oppressor's way of life—

GERONIMO. *(Interrupting.)* And with the oppressor's dick up his ass.

All laugh except Keusi.

M'BALIA. When you were in the army, Keusi, wasn't it true that a man who deserted in the face of the enemy was shot?

Keusi nods.

Well, Radcliffe has not only deserted, he has *defected*. We are at war with the beast. Don't the rules count the same here?

KEUSI. Okay, okay, okay. Radcliffe will be taken care of. But I'm doin' it with reservations. Radcliffe looks and sounds like the kind of dude who's very active in the community. Is that true?

AHMED. Ndio. More or less.

KEUSI. So that means that he's into things like sending little kids to camp in the summer and young people to college in the fall. I'll betcha he's a member of a fraternity and he's probably a deacon in his church.

M'BALIA. Yeah, the society page of *Jet* magazine. That's him.

KEUSI. That means he's probably a hero in some segments of the Black community. A lotta Black mothers are grateful to him for helping to get their sons straightened out. You got any ideas of what that means to a lotta mothers? Working in the church automatically puts him in good with the older folks.

GERONIMO. So what?

KEUSI. So, even though he acts like a Tom to us, he could be regarded as a kind of hero to many of our people.

GERONIMO. Aw, bullshit. Radcliffe's an oppressor. He's got to go. And maybe those people who believe in him will have to go, too.

AHMED. When the target is eliminated, the people will understand.

KEUSI. I'm not so sure. Once you get a rep for killing your own people, popular support starts to dwindle.

GERONIMO. It depends on what Black people you kill, an' if the nigger is an oppressor, that's his ass.

KEUSI. Who are we to decide what Black people will live and what Black people will die? We got no mandate from the people.

GERONIMO. Fuck a mandate. We the vanguard of the righteous revolution. We don't need a mandate.

KEUSI. Y'all still don't understand.

M'BALIA. Chauncey Radcliffe is an oppressor. He oppresses the Black community and he oppresses the revolution.

AHMED. Hey, man, don't worry. The people will understand.

GERONIMO. It's not the revolutionary's job to take prisoners and rehabilitate. It's the revolutionary's job to eliminate.

AHMED. The people will understand.

KEUSI. The people will only understand that we are now killin' Black people. 'Cause, see, if we kill Radcliffe then we gonna haveta eventually do away with preachers 'cause a lotta them shuckin' and jivin', too. But if we do 'way with preachers, we gonna haveta off teachers, 'cause they teachin' in the oppressor's schools, an' if we off teachers we gonna haveta start on Black government officials, 'cause they work in the oppressor's government administration an' they ain't gonna go for teachers getting' offed. We kill city and government officials, then we gonna haveta start on our families next 'cause we all got people who're teachers, preachers, civil servants, an' alla that. See what I'm gettin' at? Chauncey Radcliffe is more than just one man. He's a whole heap of people. His death is gonna open up a whole floodgate of death and destruction for Black people at the hands of other Black people. Us.

M'BALIA. When we became revolutionaries we recognized the probabilities of having to kill our own people. Even members of our own families. That's why we accepted the credo of the revolutionary, which states in part that the revolutionary can have no family outside his "family" of other revolutionaries.

AHMED. Don't forget, man. Seven Panthers are dead in this city, and three Black Terrorists are rotting in pig pens because of this one man.

GERONIMO. He's not a man. He's an oppressor. A beast. A no-thing, a non-man. His death will be of little consequence.

AHMED. His blood's gonna feed the revolution.

ANTAR. Ndugu Keusi, there is no way this man can be allowed to live. Your considerations are wise ones, but these are revolutionary times. We have to take into account the survival of the revolution. I hate to say it, but there are times when the survival of the revolution must come before the desires of the people.

GERONIMO. That's right, Keusi. The people don't always know what they want.

KEUSI. But the people *are* the revolution.

AHMED. Precisely, my brother. We articulate the desires of the people.

KEUSI. But how are we gonna do that if as revolutionaries we live

47

only among ourselves. How we know what the people want if we don't deal with their wishes?

ANTAR. We always deal with the wishes of the people. The people wished the oppressor Savage dead and we fulfilled that wish. Deep down they want Radcliffe dead. We will fulfill that wish, too.

KEUSI. But suppose the people don't want a revolution? Suppose they ain't really ready?

AHMED. That's what we mean when we say that the people don't always know what's good for them.

KEUSI. But if we represent the people, we gotta always be responsible to them. Revolutionaries are responsible to the people. If they say stop, we have to stop. We should never try to operate independent from the people. I don't know, man, but somewhere along the line I think we got a fucked-up set of values.

ANTAR. We have a correct value system, Ndugu Keusi. You shouldn't get into disparaging the revolution. Such a habit is counterrevolutionary.

AHMED. It's the same thing I was tellin' you about before, Antar. His personality and his makeup, man. Hey, Keusi, man, you gotta overcome that. You a good killer an' you got the makin's of a good revolutionary. But watch it, man. Your shit's raggedy.

KEUSI. *(Piqued.)* Yeah, yeah, yeah. Yeah, man, okay.

GERONIMO. You should recognize that the revolutionary is responsible to the people only as long as they move forward to a revolutionary position. When the people falter the revolutionary must move on ahead as a righteous vanguard, smoothing the path for the people, so that when they catch up to the revolutionary in consciousness they will see what a glorious thing it is for a revolution to put into high gear. You gotta recognize that, my brother.

KEUSI. Bullshit. A revolutionary vanguard is impossible in this country 'cause without the people the revolution is lost. Can't no revolution be successfully carried out without the support of the people. If the people don't want a revolution there ain't gonna be none. And when you get into offin' Black people as though you were some omnipotent agents from heaven or someplace then, hey,

48

man, you sealin' your own doom. "The saviors of the people must not become their tormentors as well."

GERONIMO. *(Very angry.)* We ain't no tormentors!! Goddamnit, we righteous revolutionaries!!! Just assassins! ! Black Terrorists! We *are* the revolutionary vanguard. An' we gonna keep on vanguardin' 'cause too many brothers and sisters have died to get us to this point. We goin' forward all the time!! The oppressors will die! Alla them!! 'Cause it's only right and just that they do so!! And any deaf, dumb, blind, incorrect nigger that gets in our way, gets his ass *blown* away. You understand?! His blood flows! Motherfuck the nigger! He dies!!

KEUSI. Is that all you got to offer the people, man? Death? Black people been dyin' in the most vicious manners imaginable for the past four hundred years. Hey, man, all you got to offer people who seen too much death is more death? Why we gotta fight a revolution with a value system directed toward death? Why not wage a revolution directed toward life? Huh?

AHMED. Oh, will you listen to this romantic, idealistic motherfucker?

KEUSI. I mean it. Why y'all playin' up to death alla time? Don't nunna y'all wanna live?

GERONIMO. That ain't got nothin' to do with it! If we gotta live under the yoke of oppression then we choose death. At least in death we can have some measure of freedom!!

AHMED. If it's gonna take our deaths to secure life for Black people, then we say to our oppressors, "Take our lives, if you can!"

ANTAR. We don't glorify death. We just acknowledge its inevitability. To die for the revolution is the greatest thing in life.

KEUSI. To live for the revolution is even greater. To be alive to fight the next—

GERONIMO. Aw, nigger, you just scared of death!

ANTAR. *(Comfortingly.)* To be afraid of death is nothing to be ashamed of, Keusi. It's a fear we must all overcome.

KEUSI. I ain't afraid of death. I've risked my life countless times. It's the glorifying of death I'm afraid of.

AHMED. To be unafraid of death is not to glorify it!

KEUSI. Aw, why the hell don't you niggers stop sloganeering an' come down to earth. Y'all runnin' around here talkin' about you ain't afraid to die, waitin' for a chance to die to show the world that you meant what you said. Hell, if I'm scared of death, then y'all just as scared of life.

GERONIMO. Life at the price of slavery is unacceptable! Like the motherfucker said, "Give me liberty or give me death."

KEUSI. Fucked-up references and fucked-up values.

GERONIMO. Ramon, Victor, and Juney-bugs was real revolutionaries. Brave cats who met their moment in true revolutionary fashion. They weren't cowards. Not like you. They died valiantly.

KEUSI. They died needlessly.

    Shocked gasps from others. Geronimo starts for Keusi.

GERONIMO. *(Being restrained by others.)* You spittin' on they name?! You punk!! You punk motherfucker!!

KEUSI. I don't care what you call me. The facts are there for you to deal with. They died from an overdose of revolutionary fervor.

ANTAR. Don't be impudent!!

    M'Balia bows her head in silence from this point on. She seems hurt and dismayed. After a while she should move from the group to an area by herself near the door.

KEUSI. I'm not. I'm tellin' the truth. Hey, man, I'm sayin' that if cool heads had been in charge not a single member of the ALF would have died.

GERONIMO. The enemy was tryin' to kill us. We wasn't gonna cringe in front of them. Not in front of the beast!!! We wasn't about to give them that satisfaction.

KEUSI. You had an out, man, an' either you couldn't or you wouldn't use it. You let revolutionary zeal get in the way of effective, clear thinking and blew, man.

GERONIMO. What the hell you tryin' to say? We was attacked by the pigs. We had no choice *but* to fight.

KEUSI. You had a choice, man. You had the option to postpone that battle an' you refused.

GERONIMO. You sayin' we shoulda surrendered?! Huh?! Is that

what you think we shoulda done?! Man, you must be crazy. We ain't scared of no pigs! You must be outta your mind!

KEUSI. You had a situation in which 'cause of the hour of the raid your station was undermanned. In fact, from everything I've learned about it, man, there was more sisters than brothers in the headquarters at the time. You were outarmed and outnumbered from jump street. You were in charge of the most crucial chapter of the ALF in the country because of the alliance you made with the Black Terrorists. Also, because you had built your headquarters into a fort, valuable records from chapters all over the country were stored there. Even though you had this fort everybody knew that no matter how strong the damn thing was, history showed that when the Man wants to take it, he can. You can hold him off maybe six minutes, maybe six hours, maybe even six days, but eventually the Devil can mount a successful assault. Geronimo, you knew that, and that's why the out was built. An' you didn't use it, man.

GERONIMO. Man, I didn't have no out! We was attacked. We recognized that we had to deal with the Night Rangers on the spot. We knew we might die but we knew that even in death we would set a revolutionary example.

AHMED. They gave impetus to the revolution. Ndugu Keusi, you got no right to jump on Geronimo like this.

KEUSI. Aw, man, will y'all listen to reason?! Man, everything, all the records, weapons, and personnel were lost in that battle, when the truth of the matter is that it didn't even have to happen.

GERONIMO. It had to happen! The moment dictated it!

KEUSI. You had an out, man, and because you didn't use it, the whole movement has been set back.

GERONIMO. What "out"? Whatchu keep talkin' about? Our backs was to the wall.

KEUSI. Man, don't you see? I'm talkin' about the escape tunnel.

GERONIMO. We used it, dunce! How you think me and the survivors escaped?

KEUSI. Why didn't you use it from the git?

GERONIMO. Because we had to fight! We was under attack!

KEUSI. But you was outnumbered and outarmed. You had valuable records and documents. To engage in such a battle woulda been useless. You faced losing your men, your records, and possibly capture. Hey, man, that escape tunnel was your out.

GERONIMO. We was supposed to run from some cowardly oppressors, is that it? You expect us to run like those five white boys did?

KEUSI. I expected you, as the leader, to have kept a cool head and to have looked past the emotionalism of the moment. You dig?

GERONIMO. I ain't a coward, man, an' neither was the brothers and sisters who was with me. We weren't gonna run like those white boys did.

KEUSI. In they fear, those crackers showed you just what you shoulda done.

AHMED. *(Angry.)* You takin' the side of white boys against your brother?!

KEUSI. No, man. They were even more wrong. In fact, we all know they shouldn't even have been there in the first place. They coulda created panic and confusion runnin' like they did. But they got away, man. They alive walkin' around, totally useless to the revolution, while real revolutionaries are dead because their leader wasn't able to see the need to order an orderly retreat in the face of superior firepower.

GERONIMO. Meaning what?

KEUSI. Meaning you a piss-poor leader. You was so eager to fight the Man that you ignored the safety of your warriors and overlooked the need to protect those files.

GERONIMO. Goddamnit, we was under attack by half an army. How you expect me to think of everything at once?

KEUSI. 'Cause you was the leader. Your first duty was to the safety of your warriors and to keep those records and files from being lost. You gotta think of all the contingencies, man.

GERONIMO. Look, motherfucker, I AM a leader, and a damn good one.

KEUSI. You jeopardized a whole movement when you did what you did. Revolutionary zeal got its place, man, but it's outta place in a situation like the one you was in.

GERONIMO. I'm a revolutionary. My job is to kill the enemy, foment revolution among the people, and lay my life on the line if necessary.

KEUSI. You not a revolutionary. You just an angry nigger with a gun. You filled your head fulla a whole lotta slogans and you followin' an ideal that somebody lifted from the fucked-up minds of some nihilistic white boys who lived a hundred years ago.

GERONIMO. Keep it up an' I'm gonna bust a cap in your ass.

KEUSI. You had ample warnin' when those white boys did their thing. All you had to do was put the sisters in motion, carryin' the files out through the tunnel while the brothers fired to keep the police at bay. Then when the cops made their big push, y'all coulda gone under-ground, anything you wanted. Alla y'all woulda been alive to be *living* revolutionary examples, continuing to fight, instead of martyrs inspiring young impressionable kids to copy your suicidal deeds.

GERONIMO. You sayin' we shoulda run?! You sayin' we shoulda imitated those cowardly white boys?!

KEUSI. Man, ain't you listened to nothin' I said? I'm only runnin' down to you what the V.C. did to us every day. This is how Frelimo is kickin' the Portuguese outta Africa. Hey, man, I ain't sayin' y'all gotta be cowards. I'm sayin' to calm down and use your heads.

GERONIMO. *(Still ignoring Keusi.)* I'll die before I run!!

ANTAR. Hindsight is always easy, Ndugu Keusi. The brother described the situation to us himself. We too questioned his tactics, but he correctly, we felt, pointed out to us that there is little time to take all that you said into account.

KEUSI. It don't take no time to burn some files and split. Geronimo allowed all this revolutionary zeal to get him all jammed up. The nigger got the most colossal death wish I ever seen. So does the whole goddamn revolution. We walkin' around practically worshippin' death. We so eager to die that we forgot how to live. The revolution gonna fail if we keep this up.

GERONIMO. Bullshit! The revolution can't fail. We've seized the moment. Time is on our side. We can't fail!!!! The French Revolu-tion, the Anarchists, the Bolsheviks—ain't nunna them gonna have nothin' on us!!

KEUSI. You should realize, Ndugu Geronimo, that ultimately the French Revolution has failed 'cause after all those people got their heads cut off, after the motherfuckin' Reign of Terror, after eight republics, France is still fucked up. If you gonna use the Anarchists as a reference, then study they *whole* history; didn't a single one of those cats survive the Battle of Paris in the 1850s. The French cops and the citizenry killed them by the hundreds down to the last man and stacked their bodies like logs in the streets, and the fuckin' Bolsheviks unleashed Stalin on the world. See what I mean about references! It don't seem right to me that the crazy ideology of some sick Europeans should be passed off as the revolutionary ideology of Black people. We got to offer our people life, y'all. Not more death.

AHMED. But we're talking about constructive death!!

Pause. All look at Ahmed.

KEUSI. We are preparing ourselves to fight on the basis of a foreign ideology, brothers. We usin' the politics of the pig. And if we fight on that level then that fight's gonna be a futile, royal ass-kickin' with millions of our people dead, locked away in prisons, or run out the country. I mean, if we gonna achieve some kinda change in this motherfucker we gonna haveta do it without usin' the politics of the pig. We got to use all the economic, political, and military know-how we got, but we gotta learn to use it wisely and cunningly. We got to wage our fight on a new level of thought and action. You dig? We gonna haveta run a master game down on this beast. Otherwise, Black people are gonna keep on getting wasted on bullshit hummers. We stay on this path an' we gonna fail our people.

AHMED. He's lying!!

GERONIMO. *(Drawing a gun; angry as hell.)* Motherfucker, you standin' in the way of the revolution!!

Just as he is about to fire, Antar hits his arm and the gun misfires. M'Balia screams. Antar and Ahmed restrain Geronimo, who breaks down and cries.

He's a traitor! Kill him! That nigger's blockin' the revolution! He's downin' everything we stand for. The motherfucker's destroyin' our beliefs!!

Two Terrorists rush in, guns drawn.

ANTAR. *(To the two Terrorists.)* Help this brother to his quarters.

The two Terrorists help Geronimo out.

Ndugu Keusi Kifo, I will admit that some of what you say may have a ring of truth, but I cannot and I will not condone your conduct. You have behaved in a manner that, at best, can only be described as counterrevolutionary. You are a totally undisciplined individual and I, for one, found your little act here disgraceful. For all of your supposed knowledge you still have yet to learn that it is far wiser to be constructive in your criticism rather than insulting, arrogant, and vicious. Your powers of persuasion are virtually nil. I think you're one colossal ass. In view of your attitude, I cannot trust you to carry out your mission against your other target. I'm relieving you of your responsibility to that mission. I am also suspending you from all other revolutionary activities except attendance at our indoctrination classes. I should have listened to Ahmed when he first told me of your maladjustment. You are dangerous. Despite his eccentricities, Geronimo is a very capable revolutionary leader. Your attack on him was excessive, biased, and unforgivable. I only hope these indoctrination classes will help you. If not, I will expel you from this revolutionary cadre. You're dismissed, Kifo.

> *Keusi starts out. He stops near M'Balia, who is by the door. They look at each other but say nothing. She turns from him and he exits.*

AHMED. You should have let Geronimo kill him, Antar.

M'Balia buries her face in her hands. Lights go down.

Scene 7

> *Back at the apartment, Keusi is seen packing a knapsack. After a while, M'Balia enters. She watches him a moment, then moves toward him.*

KEUSI. *(Noticing her.)* Hey, how ya doin'?

M'BALIA. Alright.

KEUSI. You come to jump in my ass, too?

M'BALIA. No.

KEUSI. Uh-huh. I'll tell you one thing. I was really surprised by them. I didn't think they were so reactionary.

M'BALIA. I didn't think you were so negative.

KEUSI. But I wasn't negative.

M'BALIA. Yes you were, Keusi. You tried to destroy Geronimo in front of the other men.

KEUSI. I tried to correct him.

M'BALIA. Insulting him and trying to undermine him is no way to get him to see your point of view.

KEUSI. I'm sorry, baby, but I got no patience with overzealous motherfuckers. I seen too much of that in the army an' I seen it get a lotta people wasted. Y'all act like the revolution is just one great big romantic gang war. It's serious business—

M'BALIA. *(Interrupting.)* Don't lecture me. I know what revolution is, and I know what death is, too.

KEUSI. Well, if you know what it's all about, then why you puttin' me down for comin' down on Geronimo?

M'BALIA. Oh, I don't know. I didn't feel you had to be as malicious as you were, but, Keusi, Ahmed wants you dead. He said as much to Antar after you left.

KEUSI. Fuck that nigger. Shit, it doesn't matter anyway. I'm gettin' out. I've had it. I would have thought that at least Antar would have seen where I was comin' from, but he's let the revolution blind him, too.

M'BALIA. You're going to run?

KEUSI. I'm not running. I don't believe in the Black Terrorists anymore. So it's just better that I split. I'll never sit in any indoctrination and listen to revolutionary bullshit that came from the minds of crazy-ass Europeans.

M'BALIA. What will you do?

KEUSI. Keep on fighting. I don't know. I heard about these brothers who are into some new concepts and ideas. Maybe I'll join them.

M'BALIA. Can we really be that wrong?

KEUSI. Baby, times change. The whole world is different. You got to be flexible. An' the Black Terrorists just ain't flexible. They so dogmatic an' shit.

M'BALIA. I don't understand you. If you feel this way, why did you join us in the first place?

KEUSI. I don't know. Maybe then I was only beginning to see things. After meeting Geronimo and after listening to Antar take my ass over the coals an' shit, I began to realize that it was time for me to split.

M'BALIA. What if those other brothers don't meet with your approval? Will you leave them, too?

KEUSI. If they bullshittin', yeah, I'll leave them.

M'BALIA. Then I guess you'll always be on the outside, Keusi. It just don't look like you can ever really find anything to believe in. As soon as something goes wrong for you, you leave. If what you say about us is true, don't you even think that maybe you should stay here and try to straighten things out?

KEUSI. With Ahmed and Geronimo both ready to kill me? You kiddin'? Naw, I'm splittin'. Maybe I'll just go into the Black community and educate the kids as to what I have learned in the world. Maybe that's the only thing I can do. But I can't stay here. Not another minute longer.

M'BALIA. Oh.

> *Pause.*

Well, goodbye.

KEUSI. M'Balia, I want you to come with me.

M'BALIA. No. You're asking me to be a traitor.

KEUSI. Please?

> *Moves to her.*

M'BALIA. I can't. The revolution—

KEUSI. You can still fight the revolution, but as the mother of my children.

M'BALIA. (*As Keusi takes her into his arms.*) I can't. Keusi, please, I'm an assassin. I've dedicated my life to what I do. Keusi, please don't. Please.

KEUSI. M'Balia, baby, baby, baby…please.

> *He kisses her. M'Balia starts to melt, but gains control and pushes Keusi away from her.*

M'BALIA. I can't go with you, Keusi. Not now, not ever. I swore my life to the organization. I won't leave them.

KEUSI. M'Balia, I love you. I want you with me.

M'BALIA. No. My life is with my brothers and sisters. Anything beyond that is not real for me.

KEUSI. Not even me.

M'BALIA. Not even you. You don't seem to understand, Keusi. I told you before that the best you could ever be was my lover. I meant that. I could never let you get into my heart. I never have.

KEUSI. I'm not leaving here without you.

M'BALIA. And I'm not going anywhere with you.

KEUSI. Then you don't know me very well.

M'BALIA. I know you well enough. If you're going to, run, but don't expect me to run with you. I'll never run from the revolution.

KEUSI. *(Exasperated.)* Goddamn!! Will you listen. Look, I'm not runnin' from the revolution. I'm runnin' from suicidal niggers who ain't got no idea of what they sayin' and doin'. Not really.

M'BALIA. We know what we're doing.

KEUSI. Is that so? When the revolution really begins and homes and neighborhoods get burned down, and blood really flows in the streets, and we face the full-scale cracker retaliation, you'll see what I was talkin' about. You'll see how far blind revolutionary zeal will get Black people living in white America.

M'BALIA. You're a defeatist.

KEUSI. I'm just tryin' to get y'all to see some truths, that's all.

M'BALIA. The revolution will be victorious no matter what you say, Keusi.

KEUSI. All we got is some semi-automatics, some carbines, some pistols, assorted rifles, knives, and a whole lotta revolutionary zeal. That little bit of near *nothing* against the baddest, most vicious war machine in the world. We have no means of stopping a police car, much less a tank. It took the local cops only twenty minutes to run Geronimo outta his headquarters. How long you think it's gonna take the U.S. government to TCB in a Black neighborhood. All the zeal in the world ain't gonna help us unless we learn to get our shit truly together.

M'BALIA. For every one of us who falls it will cost them ten oppressors.

KEUSI. So, it's gonna be that? With only forty million Black people in this country against at least one hundred million crackers we supposed to fight a fuckin' war of attrition. This ain't Asia, baby. We ain't got an endless supply of manpower.

M'BALIA. We can fight urban guerrilla warfare. *The Battle of Algiers* demonstrated how it could be done.

KEUSI. This is America, not Algiers. See what I mean about references? M'Balia, get it into your head that the revolution in America is gonna be the most unique in history. We can't imitate nobody. Not the Viet Cong, or Frelimo or even the Chinese Eighth Route Army. We got to make up a whole new revolution, 'cause unlike other revolutions we in a minority, and a highly visible one at that. All the beast gotta do is cage us in, surround us, and exterminate us, or, if he chooses, activate the McCarran Act.

M'BALIA. But we know the ghettos. They don't. We can hit and run through alleys an' all kinds of things. We could fight guerrilla war in the streets for months before the oppressor could do any real damage to us.

KEUSI. You ever walk into a police station and look on the walls in some of those offices. All over the place—maps. Maps of the city, maps of the neighborhoods, and maps of maps. The Man knows all there is to know about the Black communities of America. Don't forget, he built them.

M'BALIA. They wouldn't destroy their own property. We could always be able to fight and hold them off. Besides, if they did bomb us or try to kill the people off, world opinion would be very much against them, and they couldn't afford that.

KEUSI. World opinion didn't mean shit when America invaded the Dominican Republic. But that's beside the point. Look, as revolutionaries, we also the protectors of the people. So, how we gonna feed our people when the cracker stops sending food to the A&P? How we gonna get water to the people when the cracker turns off the water supply? How we gonna clothe the people when we take off John's Bargain Store? When we gonna get into educating the people as to how to take care of themselves in a revolutionary situation? We ain't been doin' this. All we been doin' is killin' cops, gangsters, and a few bullshit politicians, an' all that is doing is getting the cracker in the mood to make a big bust. That means our people are the ones who gonna suffer the most. An' that's all we can offer them, now, you know. Nothing but empty slogans, Pyrrhic victories, and more death. How we gonna sell them that kind of life? The kind of life we got off some dead Europeans?

M'BALIA. But we have to do *something*!! We can't just sit idly by and allow this oppression to continue. I don't know, your arguments are persuasive. You have a clever way with words. You can always make yourself sound so right, and I can't deal with that. But I know that unless we Black people take a stand and try to end this oppression, we'll never be free. We have to fight. We have to make war so that we can end this oppression and live as free men and women. How much longer are we supposed to put up with the terrible way so many of our people are forced to live?! What, are we insane or something? Are niggers a race of morons?! The Indians, the Africans, the Asians all chose to fight. No people will submit forever to oppression. So, what's wrong with Black people? No, Keusi, no more generations of Black children will be born into a country that kills and oppresses us in the manner that this does. We must have our manhood and womanhood and we must have it now, or America will simply have to die. We're going to change this world, Keusi. We're going to place human values above market values, we're going to build governments that save lives rather than destroy them, and after the destruction we bring to the evil and wickedness on this planet, after we've cleansed the world of the beast and all his lackeys and all other counterrevolutionary elements, no one will dare pick up a gun in anger again. And we'll do all this because we must, or else we'll die trying. So go on and leave. What does it matter? You were never any good to the revolution, anyway. Geronimo was right. You *are* standing in the way of the revolution.

KEUSI. Then why don't you kill me?

M'BALIA. Because those weren't my orders.

KEUSI. And that's the only reason?

M'BALIA. Yes.

KEUSI. You could kill the man who loves you that simply?

M'BALIA. Without hesitation.

KEUSI. Nothing that's happened changed a thing, huh?

M'BALIA. No. I told you in the beginning that I was a revolutionary. I've pledged my life to what I do.

> *Her mood changes.*

Keusi, if you intend to leave, just leave. I really don't want to deal with you anymore.

KEUSI. I want you to come with me. There are more ways to fight a revolution than with a gun.

M'BALIA. A gun is the only way. Keusi, tonight I'm going to have to prepare myself for a mission. I'd like to be alone. So…

KEUSI. What's the mission?

M'BALIA. Radcliffe. It'll be the ultimate test for me. If I succeed, it'll provide me with the ultimate freedom a true revolutionary can have. I'll be able to begin a whole new life after this mission. That is really something for me to think about. It'll even free me from doubts about being totally dedicated as a revolutionary.

KEUSI. I don't understand what you talking about.

M'BALIA. You don't need to.

KEUSI. Wow, killin' Radcliffe is really gonna put y'all out there. I guess I'll have to read about it in the papers.

M'BALIA. It'll be headline news.

KEUSI. *(Trying to joke.)* Don't miss.

M'BALIA. Oh, don't worry. I won't miss. I'm a very good assassin. I only miss when I want to.

KEUSI. Well, good luck.

> *Pause.*

So you won't change your mind, huh?

M'BALIA. No.

KEUSI. M'Balia, I know…I know you gotta feel somethin', baby. You gotta feel somethin'.

M'Balia says nothing.

M'Balia?

She moves far from Keusi.

M'BALIA. You meant nothing to me, Keusi. I needed a man. You were available.

KEUSI. You're lying.

M'BALIA. Why should I lie? I have no time to be lying.

KEUSI. Am I so wrong to ask you to be my wife? Is it a crime for me to want to love you?

M'BALIA. *(Trying to remain emotionless.)* You want me to make a choice between you and the revolution, and you're conceited enough to think you should come out on top. If Antar had told me to I would have killed you the minute I walked through the door. *(Voice starts to break.)* You mean nothing to me, Keusi. You have no right to do this to me. These are not the days for trying to win a woman's love. The revolution takes preference over everything.

KEUSI. I'm not asking you to give up the revolution. Fight it at my side. Come with me, M'Balia. Hey, baby, I love you.

M'BALIA. Keusi, you're a fool. Leave me alone. Please. For me, there's no such thing as love. I'm a revolutionary. There's no love, or no male, no female; there's only the revolution…and victory. Do you understand?

KEUSI. M'Balia—

M'BALIA. *(Stifles a tear.)* Get out! I mean it! Just get out of here and leave me alone! You've hurt me enough already! Leave me alone!

> *Keusi picks up the duffle bag and starts for the door. He looks at M'Balia, but she refuses to acknowledge him. As the door closes, M'Balia turns toward the door, stands silently a moment, then buries face in hands.*

Scene 8

A lonely room in Radcliffe's house. We see him seated behind a desk; desk lamp burning; busy reading, seems tired. M'Balia enters unseen…watches him awhile. Inadvertently makes a sound… Radcliffe spies her.

RADCLIFFE. *(Surprised.)* You!

M'BALIA. *(Speaks in subdued terms.)* Hello, Daddy.

RADCLIFFE. So, you've finally come home. You've been gone for a long time. No contact at all. I wanted to reach you to tell you how sorry I was…about…well, about everything.

M'BALIA. *(Quietly.)* Well, that's okay.

RADCLIFFE. Where have you been?

M'BALIA. In the city.

RADCLIFFE. All this time?

M'BALIA. Yes.

RADCLIFFE. Rhea—

M'BALIA. My name is M'Balia.

RADCLIFFE. What?

M'BALIA. My name isn't Rhea anymore. It's M'Balia.

RADCLIFFE. I see. What does it mean?

M'BALIA. It's the name of a sister who became a martyr and served as an inspiration for the revolution in Guinea.

RADCLIFFE. When did you change your name?

M'BALIA. I didn't change it. It was changed for me.

RADCLIFFE. When?

M'BALIA. A few days after I left you.

RADCLIFFE. I suppose that now you're a revolutionary, too. Like David.

M'BALIA. Yes.

RADCLIFFE. Rhea—I'm sorry, er—er—

63

M'BALIA. M'Balia.

RADCLIFFE. Yes. M'Balia. It sounds nice. Has a pleasant ring to it. *(Grins.)* M'Balia…you know you're the only child I have left. David's dead…and your mother, too. I…I don't want to see you lying dead as well. If you die violently and senselessly, like David, then what'll be left for me? What'll be left for your father?

M'BALIA. *(Unemotionally.)* Death.

RADCLIFFE. I suppose that's right.

> Pause.

I'm sorry…I'm sorry that our lives have become so dismal.

M'BALIA. Mine has been very fruitful, Daddy.

RADCLIFFE. It has?

M'BALIA. I've found peace, contentment, and at the same time, great challenges.

RADCLIFFE. But you're a revolutionary…or better, I should say, a misguided young woman.

M'BALIA. I'm not the one who is misguided, Daddy. It's you.

RADCLIFFE. You young people amaze me. You all think you know so much. You all assume your ideas and opinions are fresh and spanking new. Well, they're not, you know. They're old hat. They've been hashed about for years and nothing has ever come of them.

M'BALIA. That's because they've always been betrayed by Negroes like you.

RADCLIFFE. *(Angry.)* I do what I must.

M'BALIA. And so do I.

RADCLIFFE. Why did you come back? We're enemies now. You know how I feel about your revolution.

M'BALIA. I came back to…to…to say, well, to say…hello.

RADCLIFFE. *(Nods.)* Yes. Whatever else, you're still my daughter, aren't you? Strange, this revolution you young people are trying to foment. It's pitting blood against blood. Whatever else, whatever new name you acquire, I can only see you as my only daughter. Just as I saw David as my only son.

M'BALIA. Daddy, please…believe me. I'm only doing what I think is right. I don't hate you. But my life is dedicated to the revolution. I have to do what's necessary to continue the revolution.

RADCLIFFE. I don't understand what you are talking about, Rhea. What you are doing and what David was doing are the things your mother and I have tried to keep you from—all our lives. Believe me, I understand your frustrations—your bitterness. But to lash out at this white man is to invite your death. I grew up in the South. I know what he's like. I know what he can do. Your mother and I had to swallow pride and dignity many times just to be sure you and David had enough to eat. When I was David's age—when I was a young man, I often thought of fighting—lashing out, but integration just seemed a better way to go. If we tommed a little, it was to feed you—to give you a chance for the good life—a life your mother and I never had. I'm fighting against your revolution because I don't want to see any of you dying in the streets at the hands of trigger-happy white policemen. At least those boys I turned in will only get a prison sentence and that's better than getting your head blown off. I don't want to see any more Black women crying over the bodies of their men like I saw my mother crying over my father. I just don't want to see you kids dying needlessly and senselessly against such hopeless odds, and I'll fight anyone who tries to lead you down that path. I mean it. I'm not going to stand by and see an entire people exterminated, because of some disgruntled, misguided children who only half-read their history books!

M'BALIA. Daddy, you're hopeless.

RADCLIFFE. I'm sorry you feel that way, Rhea, but I'm going to finish the job I started.

M'BALIA. Then I guess I'll never see you again.

RADCLIFFE. *(Sadly.)* Perhaps not.

M'BALIA. *(Almost pleading.)* Daddy...

RADCLIFFE. Yes?

M'BALIA. *(Thinks better of it.)* Nothing. Forget it.

RADCLIFFE. Oh. *(Trying to make conversation.)* So, tell me, are you still keeping a diary?

M'BALIA. Oh, no. I cut that kind of thing out. It's very childish, you know.

RADCLIFFE. I thought all young women kept a diary.

M'BALIA. *(Trying to make a joke.)* I wouldn't know. I'm not all young women.

> She laughs uneasily.

RADCLIFFE. It's good to see you laugh again. I haven't seen that smile in a long time. I'd forgotten how much like your mother you really are.

> M'Balia bows her head.

M'BALIA. Mom was very…beautiful.

RADCLIFFE. She would have been proud to see you grow into such a fine-looking woman.

M'BALIA. Daddy, it's getting late. It's time…

RADCLIFFE. *(Interrupting.)* When you walk out of that door, part of me will die because I'll never see you again, Rhea.

M'BALIA. Yes… I… I know.

RADCLIFFE. Rhea, give up this madness and come back home. There is no life for any of you in the revolution. Leave there before you're killed or imprisoned. You can't cut yourself off from reality of the situation in this country. A revolution is suicide. You're a free woman. Don't be led into madness.

M'BALIA. *(Almost pleading.)* You refuse to understand. The revolution is already here. If it's madness we're into then it's a madness that will change the world! If we're so wrong to fight then you ought to recognize that we were driven to this point by your cowardice and the inhumanity of the enemy. Don't be so eager to put us down, especially since we're only doing now what Negroes of your generation have failed to do for years. Not another generation of Black children will have such an assortment of cowards and lackeys as… *(Voice chokes.)* …as…you…my father, Chauncey Radcliffe. They'll have brave men and women as their parents, who'll teach them to be true men and women. Free? I'm not totally free yet. I'll never be free until I free myself of this oppression that I have had to deal with all of my life.

> Now M'Balia looks directly at her father. Lips tighten with determination as she tries to muster up the words she must somehow bring herself to say.

And most of all, as a revolutionary, I can never be free until I'm free of you.

RADCLIFFE. What a well-rehearsed diatribe that was. *(Angrily.)* Don't you young people understand?! You're standing on our shoulders.

> *M'Balia is unmoved and, seeing this, Radcliffe becomes dejected.*

Well then, Rhea, what is it you want from your father? Money? My hatred? What do you want from me?

> *M'Balia is hesitant. Deep inside, her voice tells her not to go through with her assignment. She forces this inner voice into silence, summons up a great inner strength, and, trembling, faces her father.*

M'BALIA. Your death! Traitor!!

> *M'Balia pulls gun, fires. Radcliffe grabs head, blood oozes. He falls. Gradually the realization of what she has done strikes M'Balia. The stage turns red. M'Balia screams. We hear the voice of a radio newsman as M'Balia kneels at body of Radcliffe.*

RADIO NEWSMAN. Acting on information obtained from three prisoners, local police and state troopers today raided the headquarters of a supersecret Black militant organization, the Black Terrorists. Reports are sketchy, but news reporters on the scene have said the picture here is one of horror and chaos. Scores of policemen lie dead or injured in the streets and in other sectors of the neighborhood policemen are being pelted with rocks, bottles, and other missiles thrown by roving bands of Negro youths. Reporters on the scene have said that some policemen have shot a number of these youths, otherwise killing or capturing them all, while the Night Rangers, anti-riot unit of the police department, is now involved in the process of occupying and clearing out a number of homes in the immediate vicinity. There are indications that the area may have to be cordoned off for the quote, "safety of innocent citizens," unquote. There are no indications as to whether or not this cordoning off will cease once the operation against the Black Terrorists is completed.

> *Sounds; the reporter being interrupted.*

Uh, ladies and gentlemen, we take you to the scene of the action, live, where our local correspondent Neil Reiner has managed to get past security guards and is inside the headquarters to give us this exclusive report on the attack and probably capture of the Black Terrorists. Neil?

Sounds; gunfire, shouts, screams.

VOICE. Yeah?! Harry?

RADIO NEWSMAN. Yeah, Neil. You're coming through nicely. Can you tell us what's happening down there?

VOICE. *(Anguish.)* My God, it's awful. They're killing them all. The police are killing them all. Men, women, children—all *dead*!! All dead!! The police rampaged through the halls like madmen. They're covered with blood. They're like, like savages. Death is all around me. So far, I have not seen one Black alive. The police are killing them all. They're just shooting…it's unbelievable! I keep saying to myself; "This is America. It can't be happening! Not in America!"

In background, shots continue. We hear sounds of screams, death throughout, until blackout.

The Blacks are fighting like crazed animals. They are shouting chants and somewhere someone is beating a drum. I don't understand all this. Why are they fighting so hard?! All of this death and destruction. It's all around me!!! I can hear gunshots coming from everywhere. Blacks are dying, police are dying! Harry, it's like the death knell of America! Believe me!! My God! My God! These militants are frighteningly unreal, Harry. They seem to laugh at death. Almost worship it!! Rather than surrender, they fight on until dead! There's an escape tunnel, yet no one seems to have used it. I don't understand these people! All of this death!! Why?! Why?! Harry, there's a group of revolutionaries at the top of a flight of stairs. They're identified as Antar, Ahmed, and M'Balia. They may be the only Blacks alive in this building. They've got to surrender! They must! They *must*!

Lights on M'Balia dim.

Only death can be the final victor in this battle. Harry, these Blacks are fools. Why do they fight so hard?! They can't win. We're white! This is America, the greatest country in the world. We've proved we can survive any inner turmoil. Why do these Blacks continue?! Why would they rather be dead than alive in America. I don't understand! This is America! They can't win! They're foolish to continue. All of this violence. Harry, I don't—

Gunshots, screams, shouts.

Oh no!! Oh, my God!! They've got DYNAMITE!!!!!!!!!!!!!!!!!!!!!

Sound of explosion. Blackout.

BLACKNESS.

Peace Power Unity

PROPERTY LIST

(Use this space to create props lists for your production)

SOUND EFFECTS
(Use this space to create sound effects lists for your production)

Note on Songs/Recordings, Images, or Other Production Design Elements

Be advised that Dramatists Play Service, Inc., neither holds the rights to nor grants permission to use any songs, recordings, images, or other design elements mentioned in the play. It is the responsibility of the producing theater/organization to obtain permission of the copyright owner(s) for any such use. Additional royalty fees may apply for the right to use copyrighted materials.

For any songs/recordings, images, or other design elements mentioned in the play, works in the public domain may be substituted. It is the producing theater/organization's responsibility to ensure the substituted work is indeed in the public domain. Dramatists Play Service, Inc., cannot advise as to whether or not a song/arrangement/recording, image, or other design element is in the public domain.